Betty DeGeneres
Just a Mom

Betty DeGeneres

Just a Mom

Edited by Nancy Lamb

Foreword by Dr. Dina Bachelor Evan

© 2000 BY BETTY DEGENERES. ALL RIGHTS RESERVED.

MANUFACTURED IN THE UNITED STATES OF AMERICA.

THIS BOOK IS PUBLISHED BY ADVOCATE BOOKS,
AN IMPRINT OF ALYSON PUBLICATIONS,
P.O. BOX 4371, LOS ANGELES, CALIFORNIA 90078-4371.
DISTRIBUTION IN THE UNITED KINGDOM BY
TURNAROUND PUBLISHER SERVICES LTD.,
UNIT 3, OLYMPIA TRADING ESTATE, COBURG ROAD, WOOD GREEN,
LONDON N22 6TZ, ENGLAND.

FIRST EDITION: NOVEMBER 2000

00 01 02 03 04 ✳ 10 9 8 7 6 5 4 3 2 1

ISBN 1-55583-613-5

This book is dedicated to sons and daughters,
all beloved.

Contents

Acknowledgments

Thanks to my editor, Nancy Lamb, and to all the good people at Alyson Publications, especially Judy Wieder and Greg Constante. Thanks for your help, encouragement, and expertise. The idea for this book was theirs. I'm glad I was able to follow through with what I hope will be a helpful resource for years to come.

I appreciate all who contributed and let me share their stories in this book. Your generosity will do more good than you'll ever know.

Thanks to Dr. Dina Bachelor Evan for her wisdom and contributions.

Thanks to the Human Rights Campaign for starting me on this path of talking about unconditional love for and acceptance of our children. What a wonderful message to bring to the world. Thanks to PlanetOut and to Keppler Associates for giving me a platform to spread that message.

Thanks to all who listen and actually hear the message. It's so simple. It doesn't change. It's still just all about love.

Foreword

From the moment you become a mom, you can never not be a mom. It's an assignment that is nontransferable, nonrescindable. Even if you choose to give your child up for adoption, in every cell of your being you remain acutely aware that you are still a mom. Whether your children are infants, toddlers, tweens, or teens, you are still a mom. When your children marry and are old enough to be parents themselves, you are still a mom. When you take your last breath, you are a mom at that moment and beyond. There is no question that once you are a mom, you are forever a mom. The only question is, What kind of a mom are you?

Moms have a powerful impact in our lives, as those of us who are psychotherapists will tell you. We spend hours listening to our clients talk about their moms. If you are a mom who envisions the highest dreams for your child, I promise you that the capacity of your heart to hold an unconditional space for your child will be challenged. It may be challenged when your child dyes his or her hair purple or puts a metal ring through a belly button. It may be challenged when he or she brings home a new lover 20 years his or her senior. It may be challenged when your child wants to pursue the art of cattle branding as a career of choice. And, you can be sure, it will be challenged if your son or daughter respects you, and himself or herself, enough to tell you that he is gay or she is lesbian. That is when your heart will have to stretch. That is when your limits will get pushed. That is when your sense of self-esteem will get tested, and that is when your character will be challenged. None of it is about your child; it's all about you as a mom and the amount and quality of love you have for your child.

In this wonderful book, Betty DeGeneres has compiled touching true stories and anecdotes that will help you see the human side of this issue. More importantly, it will help you see your own humanness as well as that of your child. We live in a society that pretends to support diversity but is too slowly making progress toward living that principle. There is still much work to do, and moms can and should take the lead in this effort. Nothing less than the profoundness of a mother's love can turn the tide from hatred to acceptance and inclusion. This book contains stories that will move you to opening your heart and hopefully seeking the support you need to stand firmly with your son or daughter in his or her choice.

This book is not about sex or sexual preference. That is because being gay or lesbian is not primarily about sex either. It is about the human spirit and a choice made to demonstrate that love is not limited by gender. Moms don't love their children less because of their gender. Why should we love them less because of the gender they love?

In this heartwarming book you will read true stories about the pain and joy our children have gone through for being gay or lesbian. I say "our children" because they are all our children. The kind of world we create for them and for their children depends on our ability to love them unconditionally. Our success can be measured only by how confident, self-loving, and self-respecting our children become. When our spirits have provided the message that we love our children and the people they choose to love—without condition—this is how they will love themselves and others.

In the same way that being a mother is not rescindable,

neither is the fact that one is gay or lesbian. It can be hidden; it cannot be changed. The only thing that can be changed is our response as mothers to the fact that our child is gay or lesbian. To become more profound as mothers and as people, we must be willing to let go of our old programming about who our children must be. They are who they are—and who they are is worthy of being loved. It's a spiritual imperative, not an issue of sexual choice.

Betty DeGeneres has lived this experience firsthand, thanks to her loving, courageous daughter, Ellen DeGeneres. Their wonderful journey together has allowed these three to dance in the experience of acceptance, unconditional positive regard, and mutual respect. Their level of awareness has made them a safe haven for others to confide in and be supported by. I am sure it is their wish that your journey be as joy-filled as theirs has been. As you read this book and take this journey for yourself, remember that there is truly only one priority: Act out of love, not fear, for your child. Then you will write to Betty as I did, thanking her for being an outspoken pioneer who is helping us all to be better moms on this spiritual journey.

—Dina Bachelor Evan, Ph.D., MFCC

Chapter One

Parental Rites

> What the best and wisest parent wants
> for his own child, that must be
> what the community wants for all its children.
> —John Dewey

I remember hearing that when my friend Judy Shepard, Matthew Shepard's mother, met President Clinton, he took her aside and told her she was an inspiration to us all. He said Judy had gone out of her way to

Martha Fish

Judy Shepard and I had dinner in Los Angeles with several friends—a rare nonofficial event. Our paths have crossed several times now, and the more I know her, the more honored I am to be in her ever-widening circle of new friends.

reach out to others with passion and courage, adding that she was a fantastic role model. Judy responded simply: "No, I'm just a mom."

The story brought tears to my eyes. Although our lives

are very different, I know exactly what she meant. I feel the same way. No matter to whom I reach out, no matter where I speak, no matter who I touch or affect or change in some positive way, I am just a mom. And for that, I am grateful. I can't think of anything I'd rather be.

In the Beginning

If someone asked me to name the highlight of my life it would be the births of my two children. Nothing else comes close. Not that the act of giving birth was part of the highlight. But holding a tiny, brand-new human being in your arms obliterates the memory of pain. Which is why women do find the courage to give birth again.

Although I delighted in every age and stage of their childhood, my most treasured memories are of Vance and Ellen as babies. These days I laughingly tell new mothers, "Sit on them. They're grown up and gone before you know it."

Life passes so quickly. One day I was young, and the next time I glanced in the mirror a middle-aged woman stared back at me. As I recall, in those busy days of raising a family, I didn't have time to daydream and reflect about who these little people would grow up to be. Even if I had thought about those questions, it never would have occurred to me that Vance or Ellen could or would be gay.

Back then, being gay was the Great Unspoken, and the possibility never entered my thoughts. I didn't even know anybody who was gay. Or at least I didn't think I did.

One of the benefits of today's public dialogue about homosexuality is that we can learn to be more comfortable with the subject. While much of the talk is strident, hateful rhetoric, more and more we're hearing calm voices of reason. Since it is an unalterable, scientific fact that 3–10% of the world's population is homosexual, all parents should be aware that one or more of their children could grow up to be gay. In fact, my psychotherapist friend Dr. Jim Gordon thinks 10% is a low figure. With untold thousands of gay men and women still living in the closet, we have no accurate way of calculating how many homosexuals are not stepping forward for a head count.

Whatever the actual percentage is, we know it is significant. This fact lends support to parents who might feel they and their children are alone in their secret world. It also reinforces parents in their desire to raise children to be comfortable with who they are. I know of some wonderful instances of mothers and fathers who allow their boys to play with dolls and their girls to take apart motors. As parents, their goal is a noble one: to honor their children for being true to themselves.

Not Like Other Boys

Too many parents feel threatened if a child is not developing "normal" interests. Certainly Marlene Fanta Shyer felt threatened by this difference. She and her son, Christopher, have written a book together called *Not Like Other Boys—Growing Up Gay: A Mother and Son Look Back.*

Distressed by the differences she saw in Christopher when he was a child, Marlene went to a psychiatrist who gave her the most appalling, irresponsible, and damaging advice a doctor could ever give a mother: Do not hug your son.

Imagine the intensity of the feelings that would drive a woman to reject her child in such a way. Shame. Embarrassment. Confusion. And most of all, fear. Fear for herself and fear for her child. And fear of what others would think of her.

Although Marlene did everything the doctor told her to do to prevent her son from becoming a homosexual, Christopher grew up to be gay anyway. Because that is who he was. That is who he is. And that is who he always will be.

In Harm's Way

Our instinct as parents is to protect our children from pain, to keep them from harm's way. At its best, the world can be a challenge. At its worst, the world can be brutal. The knowledge that our child is gay brings with it the certainty that he or she will be subjected to suffering that we can neither deny nor prevent. Once our child departs the sanctuary of home, there is little we can do to protect him or her. This leaves us feeling angry and helpless. It also leaves us feeling confused. The primary reason for this is that we don't know what to do or how to help our child.

When Ellen came out to me 22 years ago, it dawned on me that my blond, blue-eyed daughter, who had experienced discrimination only in an abstract, indirect way—as it applied to other minority groups in the South—would now become a target of people's prejudice. My beloved daughter would be called names and would be the object of ridicule simply because she acknowledged who she was. My daughter now belonged to a minority group.

Twenty-two years ago, all the negatives were out there, but then it only seemed like a pervasive kind of ignorance. Today the prejudice is meaner, nastier—a vindictiveness rooted in hatred, not ignorance. It's hard to believe that most of this homophobic venom emanates from churches.

After Ellen came out to me, she started to build her career in stand-up comedy. In order to be successful in the hardball world of show business, she was convinced she had to hide her homosexuality. Consequently, I wasn't free to tell anyone that my daughter was gay.

I remember having dinner one night back then with my husband and two other couples when one of the men started in on gay people. He thought he was being very clever, and the others laughed at everything he said. I thought he was atrocious. I wanted to get up and leave. But I was stuck. I couldn't demonstrate my distaste for this man and what he said because I could not reveal Ellen's secret. I will never forget how much I hated that moment. And I will never forget how horrified I was. What makes me sad is that this kind of stupidity still happens today. Parents still sit quietly by while homophobes parade their prejudice in expectation of approval and applause.

Public ignorance, discrimination, and derogatory nicknames are familiar to all of us. None of us wants our child to be subjected to these things. Yet we're uncertain how to cope with the ramifications of our son's or daughter's homosexuality.

Usually, our first reaction is to wonder what we, as parents, did wrong. We ask ourselves if our child would have turned out heterosexual if we had followed different child-rearing rules. Were we too lenient with our son? Did we not offer our daughter enough opportunities to follow more feminine pursuits? And if we don't blame ourselves, we often search for someone else who might have caused this "problem." I heard about one mother who blamed her daughter's lesbianism on the Indigo Girls, Melissa Etheridge, Ellen, and a gay-friendly teacher—in that order. A little education on the subject can convince rational people that playing the blame game is pointless in regard to our child's sexuality. What we do or do not do does not make our children straight or gay. They are who they are. They are born that way.

I've already made it clear in *Love, Ellen* that I didn't go through that self-blame routine. That Ellen is a lesbian has no more to do with me than the fact that she has achieved major success in Hollywood. Neither of these facts is even remotely related to my skill as a parent.

Living the Meaning of Love

Although sometimes "different" just means unusual, all too often parents see signs of "differentness" in a young child that lead them to suspect the child might be gay. The first reaction is to ignore those signs. But disowning the obvious won't make the problem disappear. Neither will trying to redirect your child's attention or making derogatory remarks about gays and lesbians. Whatever you do, however you try to change the reality before you, when your "different" child grows up, you will still have a gay son or daughter.

Marlene Shyer is a perfect example of this. As she revealed in her book, she followed the experts' advice, and her son is gay anyway.

If we're lucky enough to know or strongly suspect that our child is gay when he or she is still young, it is our parental duty to ask ourselves what we can do to protect that child; what we can do to nurture him or her so he or she can grow into a whole, healthy, and happy human being.

I am reminded of the woman who wrote to Ellen after the coming-out episode. She learned her son was gay when he was 17 years old. "We're so glad he still has two years at home," she said, "so we can make him know what a great person he is." This mother did the best and most loving thing she could do when she learned her child was gay. Determined to make her son feel good about himself, she built his self-esteem, bolstered his feelings of self-worth, and let him know he would always be loved for who he is. And in doing so, she lived the meaning of love.

Fathers and Mothers

As gay youngsters grow into teens, they begin to question why they aren't attracted to the opposite sex.

This is a crucial moment in the life of a child, a moment in which acceptance and approval by parents is critical. A boy strives to measure up in the eyes of his father, and a girl works to live up to her mother's expectations.

Dr. Jim Gordon points out that the same-sex parent is the most important role model a child has for his or her future growth. In approving his child's actions and behavior, a father accepts his son and validates his maleness. A mother helps her daughter define her femaleness in the same way.

Sometimes parents forget that they wield a kind of godlike power over their children. As a consequence, it is their God-given duty to use that power with love, kindness, and mercy. Because when parents withhold their seal of approval, they can devastate their child—condemning him or her to a lifetime of living on the fringes of emotional and psychological comfort.

Sissy

A month or so ago I heard a story about a man named Stephen who grew up in privileged circumstances in New York City. His parents were wealthy and powerful members of the social elite. By the time Stephen was seven years old he was already showing signs of being gay. Instead of playing football, he liked to paint. Instead of playing Superman with the guys, Stephen liked to listen to music. For all intents and purposes, Stephen was a sissy. And his father was appalled.

To combat his son's errant tendencies, Stephen's father enrolled him in the Knickerbocker Grays, an elite military drill team that Stephen describes as a "classic snooty, WASP-y ritual with roots in the Civil War." Every Saturday morning, Stephen donned his gray wool uniform and joined his peers at the 7th Regiment Armory for endless hours of precision military drills. He marched, followed orders, and learned how to handle a rifle. He also participated in military parades and mock battles— all because his father "wanted to make a man of him." There was not one moment of this Saturday morning ritual that Stephen enjoyed. Not one moment that made him feel any better about himself.

Needless to say, Stephen was gay then and is gay now. The sad part of this tale is that in doing what his father asked him to do, Stephen was forced into understanding that his father didn't approve of who he was. Neither did his mother. Even though he is a loving and caring human being who has become an incredibly successful businessman—he has rescued more than one corporation on the brink of failure—Stephen still has this voice inside that tells him he never measured up.

The Rules of the Game

When I was growing up, there was a right way and a wrong way to do things. Few children ever questioned this. Girls played house, and boys played ball. And we all played by the rules of the game. It never occurred to me to rebel against these rules. It never occurred to me to defy my parents' wishes. I was expected to be a good little girl. And I was.

With this in mind, when I was raising my own children, I repeated my childhood experience. As a parent, I had the same expectations of Vance and Ellen as my parents had of my sisters and me. When Ellen was eight or nine years old, I automatically assumed it was time for her to go to dancing school.

Even though Ellen was very much a tomboy and wanted nothing more than to keep up with her big brother, all the other girls took ballet classes, and I thought my daughter should too. She protested loudly, and I insisted that she at least come with me to watch a class in progress. Reluctantly, Ellen accompanied me to class and watched the young dancers do their tour jetés and pirouettes. She was not impressed. That was the end of my attempt to convince Ellen to become a dancer.

We talked recently about the fact that she was such a tomboy when she was a little girl. Ellen reminded me of the picture of her when she was three or four—happily playing in cowboy boots, shorts, and a cowboy hat. I pointed out that she wore dresses to school and Sunday School and didn't seem to mind. "But I wasn't given any choice," she replied. She's right. Back then, girls didn't wear pants to school. It was unthinkable. Against the rules.

Ellen does say now that, looking back, she felt different but didn't know what to call it. She liked girls a lot and had many girlfriends. As she grew older, she says, she found girls and women more interesting than boys and men. Throughout her childhood, I remained clueless. I loved my daughter and accepted that she was a tomboy—that she wanted no part of ballet classes and that she loved her baby dolls but never, ever wanted a Barbie.

Although I was aware of Ellen's tomboy leanings, it never occurred to me that she might be gay. And it certainly never occurred to me to withhold my love and support because she wasn't fulfilling my expectation of what a little girl should be. This was my daughter, a part of my heart. I loved her. I didn't label her.

I often wonder how gay women who didn't get that essential maternal endorsement—whether they were tomboys or not—cope with their self-image. I suspect the ones who are well-adjusted and successful in life,

love, and work are the ones who had mothers who validated who they were, even if they didn't conform to tra-
ditionally feminine ways. This confirmation of self, this
testament to love, is the most priceless gift a parent can
pass on to a child.

Chapter Two

Family Matters

Know how to give gifts unto your children.
—Luke 11:13

The Power of Denial

When we label a child—and insist that he or she conform to that label—we limit growth and deny feelings. By
not insisting that a child conform to a norm, we give a
girl room to bloom, a boy room to become who he is.
Parents have to be careful when they have a child they
suspect might be gay. In their effort to offer their son or
daughter unconditional love, some parents (no doubt a

small minority) might overcompensate by assuming the child is, in fact, gay and acting on that assumption by guiding him or her in that direction. There's always the possibility that the child isn't gay; that the boy just has a gentle side and the girl is just a tomboy.

Parental assumptions about their children's sexual orientation must be handled with the greatest sensitivity. We are dealing with a child's fundamental sense of self and fundamental sense of reality. To let a child know, by word or deed, that you think he is gay when he is not is just as damaging as telling a child he is not gay when he is. Psychologists call this disparity between two realities "cognitive dissonance."

For instance, when a girl falls down and skins her knee, parents often say, "It's all right, Sarah. It doesn't hurt." Well, the fact is, the knee is scraped and bleeding and *does* hurt! At this point the young child doesn't know whom or what to trust. Her mother is telling her one thing, and her body is telling her another. Denial of either reality confuses the child because she doesn't know what to believe. Consequently, she begins to question her own perceptions about the world.

This same kind of push-pull mentality is apparent in the stories I've heard about the men and women who used to watch Ellen's show with their families. Even though they and their parents loved the show, the kids were not allowed to watch the coming-out episode, nor any of the following episodes. No doubt the children were confused about this show they had always admired. What a missed opportunity for education and discussion. And what a loss for the children.

Parents who suspect a child might be gay or who just want to teach tolerance to their kids can still watch *Ellen* reruns and now *Will and Grace*—not to mention a plethora of other shows featuring gay characters. It's through these shows that children learn that being gay is just another way of being. And that the acceptance of difference is just another way of viewing the world.

Purse Strings

Stuart Miller, the author of *Prayer Warriors*, tells a powerful story about how denial can infect a family to the point of incurable disease.

When he was a child, Stuart was especially close to his paternal grandmother, Nanny Miller. He loved to spend time with her. He especially liked playing with her handbags.

When Stuart was four years old, Nanny Miller gave him one of her old purse, a gift that became Stuart's prized possession. He treasured the hand cream and the fake diamond earrings that were inside the purse. And he treasured the image of himself carrying that purse. Stuart even has a picture of himself with it. When he was five years old, Stuart accidentally left his purse behind at a roadside restaurant when his family was on vacation. As they drove away in the car, Stuart cried and begged and pleaded for his father to turn back. But his father, relieved his son would no longer have his sissy accessory to play with, refused.

As a slightly older child, Stuart turned his back on sports and played fantasy games instead. For Halloween his brother dressed up as a cowboy, and Stuart dressed up as his mother. He confesses that he loved to go shopping with his mom and grandmother and advise them about their wardrobes and what they should buy for their homes. And yet when Stuart finally came out to his family, his father said he never had a clue his son might be gay.

There's little to say about a person who buries his head this deep in the sand, except that here is a man who prefers ignorance over truth, who actively chooses not to know. In fact, once he learned about his son's homosexuality, Mr. Miller continued to deny the reality before him by claiming that God would take care of Stuart by turning him away from his "abominable lifestyle choice." All this would come to pass, said Mr. Miller in answer to the prayers of himself and the members of his ultraconservative religious sect, the Believers Chapel.

The price the Millers have paid for this colossal denial is the loss of a loving, caring, and compassionate son. Stuart too has endured a deep and abiding loss—of a family that apparently doesn't know the meaning of unconditional love.

Conditional vs. Unconditional Love

There is nothing quite as heady—as life-affirming and exhilarating—as being loved for who we are. A friend once told me about a lover she had: "He liked everything about me. He told me I was wonderful just the way I was...which was 20 pounds overweight, unsure of myself, and just learning how to date again after the end of a 15-year marriage." My friend glowed when she told me that. "Richard loved me 'as is,'" she said. "And even though the affair ended, I don't think I've ever felt more sexy, or more beautiful and desirable and worthy, than I did with him."

This is the power of love—unconditional and whole-hearted, a gift we can give our children as well as our partners and spouses.

A friend recently told me about some parents she'd heard about who suspected their young son was gay. Without labeling the child, without encouraging any kind of behavior other than what was honest and true, the mother and father took their son to gay pride parades and other gay-sponsored events. They also took him to nongay events. Because of the wisdom and unconditional love of his parents, this gay man understood from an early age that gay is fine—and so is straight.

Unconditional love is the backbone of a healthy relationship with our children. We often mouth these words but don't always examine the meaning behind them.

Unconditional doesn't mean most of the time. Nor does it mean all the time with one small exception. Unconditional means you love your child when she doesn't please you. It means you love your child when he disappoints you. And it means you love your child when he or she gets into serious trouble.

I hasten to add, however, that unconditional love does not mean unconditional approval. We should all make this distinction clear to our children. Just because our love is unconditional, children shouldn't assume that our respect is unconditional. Love is free. Respect must be earned.

What better way to let our children know we love them unconditionally than to show them? This is easy to do when our children are infants and toddlers, dependent on us for everything. We cuddle them. We play with them. We tuck them in at night. But some parents don't live up to the gift and the promise of parenthood when they confront difficult or unexpected situations.

When the child grows up and says, "I'm gay" or "I'm changing religions" or "I'm dropping out of medical school," that's when unconditional love is tested. Granted, these might be reasons to be disappointed. But they aren't reasons not to love a child.

I recently heard about a woman who won't speak to one of her daughters because she married a man who isn't Jewish and won't speak to her other daughter because she's a lesbian. Sounds like this woman is destined for a lonely old age.

I frequently meet young women who speak to me with tears in their eyes. Sometimes they just ask for a hug. They're starved for a warm embrace from "mom," wherever or whoever she may be. These are women in need of unconditional love, even from a surrogate mom.

Surrogate mothers come in all colors, types, and mindsets. Lots of gay young people meet surrogate moms at meetings of Parents, Families, and Friends of Lesbians and Gays. PFLAG's mission is simply to provide support, education, and advocacy to gay children and adults and their families, and to the community. To find a chapter in your area, you can contact the organization at pflag.org.

I have a brochure from the Greater Boston Area PFLAG that says, "We invite you to share our knowledge, to be free from fear, and to reach out, search and discover more about being human. Parents of gay women and men are encouraged to call us to talk, ask questions, and especially to attend our rap sessions and meetings."

At a PFLAG meeting I attended not long ago, an attractive African-American woman told me that when Ellen came out on her show, she just wasn't ready for it. Then her 18-year-old daughter informed her that she was gay. This woman shook her head as if she couldn't believe this had happened to her. "That completely changed my perspective," she said. "I thought, wait a minute, my daughter's a good person. So I guess other gay people are good too."

There are lots of things parents can do to show unconditional love during the child's coming-out process and afterward. The fact that a son or daughter is gay should in no way change the family dynamic. Your child should still be included in family get-togethers and activities just as he or she always was. I can't imagine it being otherwise. Ellen has always enjoyed our family gatherings. She particularly loved to joke around with her cousin Bill, whose sense of humor is as sharp as hers. I've had many laughs just listening to the two of them. None of that has changed. Why should it? Gradually her gay friends were included in these gatherings as well. The only thing that has changed is that we now have more people to have fun with. And more people to love.

Acceptance. Tolerance. Unconditional love. These are concepts every family should regard with reverence and respect. When you and your children live these truths, you can all live a life to be proud of. And you can treat everyone in your family with the loving kindness they deserve.

Cookie-Cutter Children

Boys and girls, both gay and straight, are blessed to have parents who are strong and wise enough to allow them to be who they are—to nurture them and not feel threatened by having a child who is "different." There's a better chance for that happening today than there was even ten or 15 years ago.

When I was a child we were molded by the same cookie cutters. Boys and girls were given no choice except to be stereotypical boys and girls. No doubt this is why today we see so many men and women coming out of long-term marriages and announcing that they are gay. As little children they were so brainwashed into their roles, so convinced they had no choice except to live up to a worn-out *Leave It to Beaver* image of boys and girls, that it takes them a good part of their adult lives to learn they are paying a horrible price for living a lie.

Today, in our more enlightened society, parents have the opportunity to nurture and support each child so he or she can grow up with feelings of self-worth and self-esteem, regardless of sexual orientation. It's no longer necessary to hide. It's no longer necessary to pretend. Parents can support their children with pride and without the all-too-prevalent questions of "What will the neighbors think?" and "What have I done to cause this?" They can support their children not because they have to, but because it is the right and loving thing to do.

I exult in my relationship with Ellen and her life partner, Anne. I love and admire and respect them because I know what good people they are. Their love and caring for each other is a beautiful thing to witness.

When I hear of parents who loved and supported their sons and daughters up until the moment that son or daughter said "I'm gay," I wonder what's in their hearts and heads. Are all of their brain cells firing? Are they truly thinking for themselves? Or are they functioning on automatic pilot? Whatever the reason for their actions, they're missing out on a lot of love.

The Price of Difference

However idealistic and optimistic my words might sound, there is a substantial part of the population that

Betty DeGeneres

Ellen and Anne getting ready for a premiere

has not yet gotten this message. I know young women whose mothers still insist that their daughters conform to some preordained idea of what is feminine. And I know young men whose fathers still insist that they "act like a man." You know the drill: Girls can't be aggressive and boys can't cry.

As if it's not bad enough that children have to deal with the outmoded expectations of their parents, they also have to deal with the current expectations of their friends. Peer pressure is a powerful equalizer. And when a child does not fit in, peers can be merciless.

One young man named Hank recently wrote me a letter about his high school experience. "I went through eighth grade majorly depressed," he said. "I didn't want to be gay." His homosexuality presented even more of a problem because he was a Mormon. Outwardly, Hank adjusted well. "I went from being a fat funny guy in middle school to being a popular class president in high school. But none of the kids knew who I was. I was sure that if they knew I was gay, I would still be that fat funny guy in the corner."

The behavior of children toward "outsiders" can range from indifferent to brutal. At the extreme we experience the horrors such as the massacre at Columbine High School—boys reacting violently in response to being marginalized. Pushed by their parents and dismissed by their peers, kids can commit horrific acts. It's up to parents to help their troubled children, to stay in touch and be aware of what's happening in their child's life so they can prevent such tragedies from occurring. This means parents and teachers can't afford to ignore disturbing signs. Nor can they pretend that everything is fine, just fine, when it is not.

Parental Self-Esteem

The problem is that when parents have kids who are different, kids who are labeled as "losers" or "geeks" or "sissies" or "weirdos," they, as parents, are often as uncomfortable with this label as their children are. I suspect that parental self-esteem plays a greater role in how parents react to their children's problems than we would like to admit.

We all want to have kids who are winners, kids who are liked and admired by their peers and respected by their teachers. We love to bask in the reflected glory of our children's accomplishments—even though the credit rightfully belongs to our children. It's a compliment to us when our sons and daughters excel. Their success is our success. When parents accompany their daughter to a soccer game and she kicks the winning goal, the parents of the girl are congratulated along with their daughter. When a boy wins the English literature prize at high school graduation, the boy's parents can also claim credit in the eyes of others for their son's outstanding academic achievement.

We feel good about ourselves when our child is honored. We sense that people think better of us as parents and as people, and we're perfectly happy to accept credit for raising such an exceptional son or daughter.

Public approval lifts our spirits and bolsters our self-esteem.

Conversely, when our son or daughter is scorned or dismissed or rejected, we're aware of the silent assumption floating in the social ether that says we must have failed in our parental duties to have produced such a difficult, ineffectual child. We feel the negative judgment of others and consequently feel awful about ourselves. Our children are, after all, flesh of our flesh, blood of our blood, extensions of our worth, our values, and our lives.

When parents are confronted with a struggling child, they are forced to confront their own inadequacy. The best thing parents can do in such a situation is make a conscious effort to separate their feelings about how their child is regarded from their feelings about themselves. It's only natural that those "What will the neighbors think?" insecurities come into play here. Some parents might even wonder if their child's being gay is their fault—or, scarier still, that they themselves could harbor some latent gay tendencies.

If parents can just step back, take an honest look at themselves, and remove their own sense of self-worth from the equation, they might then be able to give their child the love and support he or she needs to weather the chaos of the peer-pressure storm.

Sibling Stuff

Just as there is a whole range of reactions from parents who learn their child is gay, there is also a range of reactions from siblings who learn their brother or sister is gay. I've heard every combination. After one speech I gave, a mother and her twin daughters came up to me and one of the girls said, "This is my gay sister, and we love her very much!"

After another of my speeches, this one at a Southern university, a gay man told me he's one of 14 children. "With so many brothers and sisters," he said with a smile, "it took me two years to tell all of them I was gay." Without exception, every one of his siblings accepted who he was.

I met a woman in New Orleans at a PFLAG reception who told me that she has six children, one of whom is gay. All the siblings are OK with this, she said, except one who refuses to accept that someone in his family is gay. Their mother told me this story with sadness and exasperation in her voice. I had the feeling she thought there was nothing she could say or do that would change her son's mind.

I feel blessed to tell you that from the moment he heard Ellen was gay, my son, Vance, accepted and supported his sister. In fact, I asked him again recently if he

A special highlight of a "highlight of my life" evening: Vance, Ellen, and Anne presented me with the Human Rights Campaign's Civil Rights Award at HRC's National Dinner on October 9, 1999.

could remember any details about those early years after Ellen had come out of the closet. He E-mailed me his answer: "You and I talked about this before, and I told you that I have no recollection of how Ellen told me she was gay. Maybe I just sort of knew. Can't remember. And I don't remember how I reacted. It certainly wasn't a shock, but I just don't remember. As I told Diane Sawyer, I can't imagine that I was ashamed. Sorry I can't be more helpful."

Vance has no need to be sorry at all. I'm delighted by the fact that Ellen's coming out was such a nonevent for my son that he can't even remember how or when it happened. This is the way it should be, and I'm proud of Vance for his loving response and his generosity of spirit.

Chapter Three

Standing Up and Standing Out

The tough-minded...respect difference. Their goal is a world made safe for differences.
—Ruth Fulton Benedict

Double Takes

Little by little, ignorance about homosexuality will fade away as more and more parents allow their children to be who they are. The long-term advantages of this new openness are bound to have an effect on all of us. The

public benefit of not demanding that gay men and lesbians live a lie is that everyone, gay or straight, will be living in a country that has an increasing number of well-
adjusted men and women.

Children raised in homes where difference is celebrated rather than denigrated are fortunate indeed. I know
several children who are growing up in families like
this—their parents or parents' friends are gay, nongay,
and of different ethnicities and religions—and the children accept this variety as a natural part of life. And as a
welcome part of living.

In the light of all this progress, you would think gay
kids no longer have to worry about coming out. But along
with our expanding knowledge and our more open attitudes, I see signs that the conformity of my childhood is
making a comeback in some areas of the country. As our
society becomes more multicultural and diverse, gay men
and women are less inclined to play hide-and-seek. A cul-
tural backlash is forming around this hard-earned right
to be free. The hostility toward gays and lesbians isn't
manifested merely in verbal assaults. FBI statistics reveal
that murder and violent crimes against gay people have
doubled between 1990 and 1998, though I suspect that
changes in reporting procedures must be factored into
this increase.

Our Bedrock Beliefs

We celebrate the birth of this country in the tales of the Puritans who first came to America. In admiring their exploits, we tend to forget that these people demanded a rigid adherence to their religion and that failure to adhere to these strict moral standards was harshly punished. One only has to think back to the horrors of the Salem witch trials.

In spite of this ominous beginning, the spirit of our country—originated in the Declaration of Independence and formalized in the Bill of Rights—is grounded in the myth of the "rugged individual," men and women who braved stormy seas to live in a country free from the social and economic oppression of European monarchies. The generations that followed these pilgrims gave life to this spirit in unimaginable ways. Pioneers crossed endless prairies in covered wagons. Adventurers risked life and limb to chart unknown lands. Laborers toiled to build roads and railroads and telephone lines. And men and women struggled and died to defend their civil rights. The common thread that weaves through all of these stories is courage—the courage to stand up for convictions, to explore the unknown, and, against all odds, to do what is right.

The cowboy, the mountain man, pioneers in science

and industry, astronauts, ball players, presidents, artists, writers, doctors, nurses, firefighters, and civil rights leaders: These heroes—most of them unsung—are ingrained in the American psyche. We admire their courage. We cheer their memory. And yet today, in our lack of tolerance for difference, we fail to live up to their vision and we forget to honor their dreams.

Sometimes I wonder about the dark side of being a hero, how a daring and resolute man or woman can be brought low by people who take a perverse kind of pleasure in searching out and crushing the courageous. Much as we would like to deny it, the spirit of the Puritans and their witch trials still infects our national psyche, compelling us to damn the outsider and destroy the nonconformist. It's as if we cannot tolerate the idea that someone could stand so tall above us, could reach higher than the rest of us. We cannot tolerate the disparity in our stature, so we must cut heroes down to our size.

How else could we justify denigrating an entire population? How else could we torment a man because he is different or a woman because she is at odds with what we consider the norm?

As Nelson Mandela said, "There's nothing enlightened about shrinking so that other people won't feel insecure around you. We were born to make manifest the glory of God that is within us. It's not just in some of us—it's in everyone! And as we let our own light shine, we unconsciously give other people permission to do the same. As we are liberated from our own fears, our presence automatically liberates others."

It takes courage and strength of character to be who we are in a country that asks us to conform to what others think we should be. In spite of our nation's surprising puritanical drive toward orthodoxy, many of us still harbor a quiet admiration for men and women who live up to the American myth, who manage to assert their individualism in the face of overwhelming pressure to bow to the gods of convention. We root for the underdog, come-from-behind, what-a-miracle hero. We secretly cheer the man or woman who has the fortitude to march to the beat of his or her own drummer.

And, if we are to be honest with ourselves and consistent in our thinking, we must include vast numbers of gay men and women in this hallowed group. More often than not, gay people must struggle to achieve their identity. And they must fight to be who they are. These acts of courage deserve our praise and our respect. They also deserve our support.

Sooner or later the stories of gay men and women will be included in our national myth. And sooner or later gay men and women will be fully welcomed into our American family. It's our obligation as citizens and our duty as human beings to make this happen.

School Troubles

Often our intolerance of difference shows up by the time a child enters kindergarten or first grade. Until that time boys and girls can be shielded from the cruelties of other children and the insensitivity of teachers. When they enter school, however, gay children are forced to confront the reality of who they are and how other kids respond to them.

"I was always teased about being different," one young man wrote to me. "I don't think people ever knew what was special about me. I became very shy, and when I was a little older, I became depressed. I really wanted to fit in. I didn't have many friends when I was in school, and I still don't."

In March of 1999 I spoke at a university in upstate New York where I met Kyle, a young man who has known he was gay since he was 15 years old. Kyle attended parochial school for ten years; he talked to me about the teachers he encountered who thought nothing of making homophobic remarks, such as calling one of the students a "pansy" or a "faggot."

Kyle told me of one little boy who was not as "manly" as his teacher thought he should be. The boy was constantly berated with remarks such as "Oh, Robert, don't be so limp-wristed." Another teacher, who was a

Brother—a member of a Catholic teaching order—used to make derogatory, off-color remarks about kids he suspected were gay.

Still astounded five years later, Kyle told me about a comedian who came to their campus to perform. He asked if anyone in the audience was gay. Needless to say, not one young man raised his hand. That scientific survey taken, the comedian proceeded to tell painful and demeaning jokes about homosexuals.

"After a while," Kyle said, "things like that can break your spirit."

The comedian, by the way, was black.

What Parents Can Do

The parents of gay children often know their son or daughter is having trouble at school, but they don't know what to do about it. Deciding whether to interfere or to stand back is a delicate matter, one deserving careful consideration.

If your child is being picked on by other kids, sometimes you can talk to the parents of those kids. But this is a risk, one that could backfire if the parents have no sympathy for your child. It's probably a good idea to find out as much as you can about these parents before you call and talk to them.

Speaking to the teacher is another option. But there's a multifaceted dilemma that has to be considered here. If the teacher isn't sympathetic to your child, confronting the teacher could cause problems between your child and his teacher. On the other hand, not talking to the teacher could leave your child open to further peer abuse. One way or the other, the teasing and bullying has to stop, and a teacher is usually the one who has the power to accomplish this.

I would suggest that you do everything you can to keep this dialogue with the teacher confidential. If your child's classmates get wind of your actions, your interference could embarrass your son or daughter. The kids will accuse him of needing his mommy to defend him.

If your child is having serious problems at school, you should also talk to a school psychologist, if your school or district is lucky enough to have one on staff. These professionals can help you negotiate the people problems as well as the psychological ones. If conversations with parents, teachers, and other professionals fail to provide results, talk to the principal. Persist until the problem is solved.

Children are vulnerable. Even if they are blessed with loving parents and a strong sense of who they are, kids are fragile. Torment by their peers can destroy their self-confidence and break their spirit. It is our job as parents to do what we have to do to protect our children—even if it means transferring schools.

The Bully

If your child is being tormented at school by a small group of kids, or even one particular kid, one option you might consider is talking to the principal about instituting a program specifically designed for situations such as this. Wellesley College in Wellesley, Mass., has developed a special curriculum for schools to use in kindergarten through third grade. Called "Quit It," the program consists of a series of lessons that include writing exercises and teacher-led discussions. The program focuses on identifying and dealing with bullying and teasing.

On a personal level, it's a good idea to do everything you can to teach your son or daughter strategies for dealing with bullies. This is particularly hard with younger children because they can't fully grasp the psychology of the bully. It's hard for a boy to understand that the kid who picks on him at school is usually someone who is picked on at home; that the bully acts out his frustration by mimicking the abuse he receives from others.

Whether they understand the psychology or not, younger children can usually work with the idea of feeling big as opposed to feeling small. Explain this issue of self-esteem to your child, then give her the words to use the next time the bully confronts her. Tell your daughter that the child who torments her is trying to make herself feel bigger by making someone else feel smaller. Suggest that she try to verbalize these thoughts in front of other kids who can act as potential allies. There's a chance the other children will be sympathetic if they understand what is going on.

Practice with your child ahead of time. Coach her on what to say. "You're just picking on me because you feel rotten about yourself." "You're just tying to make yourself feel bigger by picking on someone smaller than you." "Why don't you pick on someone your own size and make it a fair fight?"

The object is to undermine the power of the bully without provoking him further. Knowing how to defend yourself in a variety of circumstances is important. You might even want to consider enrolling your child in a self-defense course if you think he or she can handle it.

The Reality of Depression

Sometimes the weight of the taunts and humiliations of teasing can overwhelm a child. A woman I know recently told me the story of one of her favorite childhood friends. She met Tommy in second grade when she transferred to his school. He was feminine looking and feminine acting. And he loved to draw and paint. He and my friend spent a lot of time together playing and dreaming of what they would be when they grew up.

In fourth grade Tommy wrote and produced a three-act play of *Little Women*. This experience convinced him that he was going to be a great writer someday. But with all his talent, with all his skill and ambition and vision, Tommy was mercilessly picked on for being different, for being a sissy. He never played rough-and-tumble games at recess. And when all the kids had to play dodge ball together, the boys always threw the ball harder at Tommy.

In sixth grade my friend moved to another school in another part of the city. That same year, at the age of 11, Tommy killed himself.

We hear a lot about high school kids committing suicide—kids in the throes of adolescent turmoil. Often drugs and guns, combined with love troubles and family problems, are involved. As tragic as these stories are, we can at least make some vague sense of them. Teenagers are old enough to feel the pain of their lives. Yet they're too young to understand the dreadful ramifications of committing such a horrendous act.

But when younger children kill themselves, we are dismayed in a deeper kind of way. Seven to 12-year-olds are innocents, we think. They have yet to be exposed to the cruelty of the world. There's nothing in their lives that could compel them to kill themselves. Surely things aren't so bad for gay kids that they would want to commit suicide. This is simply not true. In fact, the opposite is true. According to the March 20, 2000, issue of *Newsweek* magazine, "A 1997 study of Massachusetts high school students found that 46% of the gay, lesbian, and bisexual kids surveyed had attempted suicide in the last year."

A school psychologist told me that childhood depression is more prevalent than we think. And it is a more serious problem than we imagine. Often depression in young children is masked by symptoms that are easily misinterpreted. It's easy to acknowledge that a child might be depressed if he retreats into a shell or withdraws from his family and friends and wraps himself in silence. But there are other signals of depression that are not as obvious. Children might become excessively accident prone. They might turn into out-of-control risk takers. Or they might have angry outbursts, sometimes directed at others, but other times, more dangerously, at themselves.

As painful it is to consider the problem of depression in young children, parents cannot afford to ignore it. The consequences of doing nothing are unspeakable. And taking positive steps could save your child's life.

The bottom line is this: Countless kids who are gay speak of living with intermittent or constant depression. A child can be considered a suicide risk when the darkness closes in and it is accompanied by a prolonged sense of helplessness and hopelessness. If you are in doubt about the psychological well-being of your child, seek professional help before it's too late.

Tolerance Begins at Home

We each carry a responsibility for the welfare of our children. This means that we must not only try to protect and care for children, but we also must guide them and teach them that it is their obligation to treat all human beings with respect.

When I try to think of ways to teach tolerance to children, I can't think of a better example than this scene from "Miss Conception," the short film for HBO that Anne Heche wrote and directed, with starring roles for Ellen and Sharon Stone. Ellen and Sharon play a loving, committed lesbian couple who want very much to have a baby. They like to go to a neighborhood preschool, sit on the hood of their car, and watch the children play. In one scene a mother is leaving the school with her baby and her five-year-old daughter. Ellen and Sharon tell her what a beautiful child she has, and the mother asks them if they have kids. When they answer no, she says, "You should try it. You'd be great." The message to her five-year-old is clear: Two women who look like they love each other very much should be able to love a baby of their own as well.

A perfect real-life example is a story I heard recently about David and Aaron, two young men who went to Yosemite's fabulous Ahwahnee Hotel to celebrate the new millennium.

After dinner on New Year's Eve (a formal event, with attendees wearing tuxedos and long gowns) the two men were sitting in the lobby, and one had his arm around the other. A woman walked by with her two preteen children and looked at the men. She leaned down, touched David's knee, and said, "You two look so cute together." Her son and daughter looked at the men sort of funny and kept on walking. David and Aaron looked at each other and shook their heads.

The moment I heard that story, my response was immediate and visceral. There's no need to take offense at this woman's behavior. As a mother I know exactly what she was doing. I just wish I had had the good sense to do something like that with Ellen and Vance when they were little. It might have made a world of differ-ence. Ellen could have seen my attitude toward same-sex couples and embraced who she was with confidence instead of insecurity. And she might not have been so frightened about coming out...so frightened about telling me, and then the world, who she really is.

As all mothers and fathers know, there's nothing kids hate more than a good parental lecture. No matter how sincere, no matter how heartfelt, no matter how well-intentioned, children rarely learn from teacher tactics. When I think back on all the rolled eyes I got as a parent, on all the "Oh, no, here she goes again" glances passed between Ellen and Vance, I wish I could replace every one of them with a more positive—and receptive—response.

The woman in the Ahwahnee Hotel was showing her children that she approved of these men's behavior and considered it delightful. She didn't take her son and daughter aside and point to David and Aaron, offering a minilecture on the different kinds of sexuality and what it means to be gay and isn't it nice that those two handsome young men cuddling on the sofa could do that without someone calling them names. Instead, she showed her children through her actions that what they saw was good and welcome and normal. Trust me, those two children got the message. And their mother didn't need to say another word.

Which brings me to the larger issue of how parents

can educate their children—gay and straight—when they are young and curious and receptive to positive, loving messages.

1) If you have gay family members, be sure to include them in family gatherings. And be sure to invite their partners. I have a straight friend who recently celebrated her 60th birthday. Fifteen people came to the party, four of whom were gay. This is the norm in that family, not the exception. And nobody, including her two sons, thinks anything about it.

2) Don't treat your gay brother-in-law or lesbian aunt as a family secret. And don't allow some of the relatives to whisper about Cousin Eddie. Children are emotional and intellectual sponges. They pick up the attitudes of those around them. If you have a gay friend or family member, that fact should be noted publicly but casually. No big deal.

3) It goes without saying that you shouldn't allow the use of derogatory epithets for gay people or anybody else. If you hear your child calling someone a "faggot" or any other such name, you should put a stop to it immediately. Furthermore, if you are with your children when someone else uses language like that, you can turn the situation to your advantage by commenting on the ignorance and ugliness of the remark. And

Betty DeGeneres

Memories of Thanksgiving 1998: Cameras, cameras everywhere—Vance with video, Anne with still, Ellen attacking the turkey with Anne's Psycho knife, and I captured it all.

if the opportunity is right to do it, you can confront the name-caller. The point is that you should not let a remark like this pass without saying something.

All of these things—from making a casual comment to a gay couple to not allowing denigrating epithets to be used in your family to treating people with fundamental respect—create the loving and accepting atmosphere that makes everyone feel welcome. And they show children a kinder way to walk through a confusing and challenging world.

Chapter Four

Coming to Terms

There is nothing so powerful as truth.
—Daniel Webster

Teen Turmoil

By the time they're 10 years old, most gay kids have begun to get the idea that they are more than just "different." Girls watch their friends turn their attention to boys, and they don't understand what the fuss is all about. Boys start to hear talk about making out with girls, and they want to make out with boys instead.

As one young woman said to me, "I first knew I was

gay in kindergarten. At recess a group of us would collect dandelions from the schoolyard for wedding bouquets. Then we would line up to be married. I always wanted to marry the girls."

By the time kids reach their early teens, words like *faggot*, *homo*, and *dyke* begin to work their ways into the school yard vocabulary. Often children don't know what those words mean. They just know they're bad—and something they don't want to be.

For some gay boys and girls at this age, the mere act of going to school can take on aspects of the heroic. Everyday, gay kids run the emotional gauntlet set up by their peers. If they're lucky, they have parents who love them, friends who care about them, and teachers who support them. But often they do not.

Beginning in the preteens, the kids who usually pay the highest price for their differentness are the small, delicate boys. They are the easiest targets for malice. And they are usually the kids who suffer the most for their orientation.

A young man named Tom wrote to me about his recent experience. At his first school, he said, "I would walk down the hall and be stared at and commented on openly. The administration did little to alleviate the situation and blamed me for my problems. They said I was 'stirring the pot' and looking for attention with the way I dressed."

Tom recently transferred to another school, but his life is still difficult. "This semester has *not* been good for me," he says, "and I'm not ashamed to say I have been depressed and suicidal on and off. Worse than the bashing is the loneliness, the continual berating. The stigma of associating with 'the fag' has pretty much sent my social life into a coma."

Studies indicate that gay kids are five times more likely than straight kids to feel unsafe at school and seven times more likely to be threatened or injured with a weapon. This statistic is realized in the stories I read, the mail I receive, and the conversations I have.

My friend Craig says he's always known he was gay. His earliest memories are of understanding that he wasn't like the other kids. He just didn't know what the difference was, where it came from, or what to call it. He describes himself as being small and pretty. Bigger boys picked on him all the time. Every night Craig said his prayers. And every night he asked God to show him what it was that people saw in him that he couldn't see—what was it that made the other kids call him names and be so mean to him.

By the time Craig was a preteen, he figured out that he wasn't big enough to beat up the bullies. But he could outrun them. Speed became his key to power and dignity.

When Craig reached junior high school, the coach who had called him derogatory names in the past noticed Craig's talent. Eager to have such a fast runner represent the school, the coach asked Craig to join the track team. Words like *faggot*, *sissy*, and *pansy* crossed Craig's mind as he looked at the coach and smiled. In a moment that must have felt as sweet as it was vindicating, Craig respectfully declined the invitation. Then he took the time to remind the coach of his cruelty, saying he would never do anything to support such a bigot.

A New Connection

A friend of mine says she realized she was gay when she was in the fourth grade and developed a crush on the girl across the street. By that age—ten—a lot of gay kids begin to understand that they aren't like their peers. They're not always certain what it is that sets them apart. But they do have an acute sense that their otherness should be kept a secret. This differentness that has no name is a source of embarrassment and, worse, a source of shame.

A farm boy who grows up on the plains of North Dakota rarely has the opportunity to learn that there are other boys in the world who have thoughts like his. It's likely he tries everything in his power to keep his feelings a secret. This, of course, makes him feel more alienated, the classic stranger in a strange land.

Today, however, with the advent of television and computers, gay kids aren't as isolated as they were in the past. The Internet provides gay children with a source of community in an otherwise alien world. Chat rooms and support groups can give kids the feeling that they're not alone. Books too address subjects that once were forbidden. All these resources give gay kids new avenues for discovering who they are and how to cope. Yet even with this help, they still need the approval of their peers and the love of their parents. Without this, they suffer.

Raging Hormones

Ask any of your friends about their adolescence. Ask them if they'd go back and do it over again—without knowing what they know now. In my experience, more men than women answer yes to that question. But the majority of answers from both sexes run along the line of, "Are you kidding? There's not enough money in the world to make me be an adolescent again."

By the time they reach junior high and high school, the vast majority of gay kids know they are homosexual. That doesn't, however, mean they know what to do about it. In today's more open social environment, a growing number of kids find the support to come out. But too many gay children continue to hide their feelings. They're not certain how to cope with this assault on their senses, and they're insecure about finding out. All they want is for these feelings to go away.

I suppose Ellen is fortunate in that she was spared these confusing feelings of being "different" at an early age. She has told me that she had her first homosexual experience when she was a senior in high school.

"This was a harmless kind of friendship/curiosity thing," Ellen says. "It didn't feel like, 'Oh, this is who I am.' I even had a boyfriend at that time. I thought it was because we were close friends. I didn't think of it as a lifelong decision."

This was just Ellen's good friend, as far as I knew. They seemed very happy to be together—extremely companionable. Now I know why!

At best, adolescence is a challenging time. At worst, adolescence is a nightmare. We're no longer children, but we're not grown-ups either. We're adrift in the netherworld between dependence and responsibility. One moment we're a child. The next moment we're an adult. And we don't have a strong grip on being either.

Add to the raging hormones and emotional chaos the alienation and confusion of being gay, and you've got a recipe for disaster.

By time children reach their mid teens, being popular
has long since moved to the top of their "To Do" list. And
having a boyfriend or a girlfriend becomes a priority. But
what if the boy wants a boyfriend and the girl wants a
girlfriend? When the stirrings of sexuality are directed
toward the same sex, the difficulty and confusion of adolescence can be multiplied a thousandfold. It's a wonder
that any gay kids survive this tumultuous time.

As I said before, young people today are often eased
into their feelings with the assistance of Internet chat
rooms and support groups. Even a kid living on a ranch
in the wilds of Montana can access the World Wide Web.
But wider communication still does not completely ease
the confusion that most of these children are feeling.

As they struggle inwardly with who they are and outwardly with who they'd like to be, gay kids are harassed
and questioned from all sides. I heard from one high
school boy named Zach who tried to be quiet about his
homosexuality. A friend cornered him and asked him if
he was gay. "You never talk about girls," he accused. Zach
managed to avoid a direct answer, but he was shaken by
the question. Soon, he knew, he would have to declare
himself before someone else did it for him.

A young woman named Felice told me she'd known
she was gay since she was 14 years old. Before coming
out, she struggled with her identity for more than two

years, trying her best to like boys instead of girls, to join in conversations with her friends about who she thought was the cutest boy in class, and to do all the other things that teenage girls do. The issue of self-acceptance is the central one for all of us. For gay kids, it is critical. But beyond her internal struggle, Felice was afraid of what would happen to her social life once her sexuality had been declared. She worried that her openness would scare away her friends or, at the very least, distance them. And she was afraid of what her friends' parents would say.

Horror Stories

We, who are heterosexual, can only imagine what gay young people experience. What's particularly sad, as in the two cases mentioned above, is that gay children must wrestle not only with the trauma of adolescence but with their sexual orientation—and that for the most part, they must do so alone. Worse, they are sometimes severely punished for their feelings.

A young woman recently told me that when she came out in high school she was threatened with not graduating, was beaten by other students, and had her house vandalized. She managed to graduate anyway. But she still gets harassed by her former classmates.

A young man wrote and told me that when he was 15 years old he came out to two friends. These two kids told other kids, and soon the whole school knew. Now, two years later, people keep asking him about being gay—how does he know, what is he doing about it, does he have a boyfriend? Instead of feeling more comfortable with himself, the boy is now constantly on guard.

Another young gay man told me about how much he loves to play football. He lives his life in the open and is on the high school football team. "A lot of kids accuse me of playing football so I can look at the guys," he said. " 'If that were true,' I tell them, 'it would be much better if I were the manager of the team. That way I could look at guys all the time. The fact is, I love to play football.' "

The saddest story I know is that of a woman who wrote to me about the isolation and confusion she felt as a child.

From as far back as the first grade, even though I didn't know what being gay was, I had a conscious and growing awareness of the difference between me and what seemed like every other girl I knew…. As a twin, I grew up with a sort of mirror image of what it was I was supposed to feel and be like, an image I couldn't live up to…. I remember an experience in junior high when I was surrounded by a group of boys in front of a locker and called a 'lezzie.' I felt as if I were frozen against that locker...as if someone had ripped something from inside of me. I was left with a name and feeling of shame for who I already knew I was. Like it or not, I was stuck with her. Until that day, I thought it could always be my own secret. I was scared to death to think that it was something others could actually see or know about me. Out of fear and shame I worked to make sure my family, who I thought would be devastated by this, would never know this about me.

Imagine the pain and loneliness and isolation this child felt. Nobody knew her. Nobody knew who she was, how she thought or what she loved. Then multiply those feelings by hundreds of thousands of children all around the world.

Lifesavers

In all of these cases, an enlightened teaching staff, a gay-straight alliance, or PFLAG members speaking to the school could change the life of these teens. Such an educational resource would go a long way in helping straight kids learn to accept their gay friends. And it could give gay kids the courage and support they need to accept who they are.

There are several ways young people can find help

when their lives become too painful and confusing to cope. The National Youth Advocacy Coalition is a terrific support group that reaches out to teens in trouble. They can be contacted through E-mail at nyouthac@aol.com.

Other organizations, such as the Gay, Lesbian, and Straight Education Network, have become excellent resources for kids. GLSEN, founded in Massachusetts in 1990 by Kevin Jennings, became a national organization in 1994 and is now based in New York City. GLSEN works to ensure equal treatment of all students. Its Web site, GLSEN.org, offers a wealth of materials from *Just the Facts About Sexual Orientation & Youth: A Primer for Principals, Educators & School Personnel* to *How to Start a Gay-Straight Alliance.*

Directions for how to start a gay-straight alliance and the reality of establishing one are still a long way apart. Recently, Salt Lake City has been the location of one major fight to establish an alliance. In November 1999 a federal judge ruled against the establishment of a Salt Lake City alliance after the school board decided to eliminate all extracurricular clubs rather than have an organization on campus that addressed gay issues.

And Orange County, here in Southern California, has been in the headlines recently because a federal judge ordered the Orange Unified School District to allow a gay-straight alliance—founded by a courageous young man named Anthony Colin—to meet at El Modena High School in Orange. Writing in *Newsweek* magazine, Harriet Barovick says the parents opposed to this ruling were the ones who spoke the most explicitly about sex at the school board debates. And, I might add, they were also the ones who were most ignorant about homosexuality. "In El Modena, as part of their arguments," Barovick reported, "they [the parents] brought up graphic details of pedophilia, bestiality, anal sex, and…'how gay people all have AIDS.'"

The judge cautioned that education officials should not act as "thought police" over controversial student speech. In his ruling the judge wrote about "tolerance for diverse viewpoints." His is a voice of reason amid the hysteria of misguided educators and parents who espouse hatred and teach intolerance.

The rational response to this judgment in Orange County was expressed recently in a letter to the editor of the *Los Angeles Times.* "It is better than strange that antigay protesters chanted 'protect the children' outside a Santa Ana courthouse. That's exactly what the judge inside did as he granted the gay students and their straight friends the right to meet on school property."

Where to Go for Help

There are, of course, many cases involving gay children and teens that merit immediate and critical attention—cases in which a child's life is at risk. Nationally, the suicide rate for teens is appalling, and 30% of those teens are gay. In Los Angeles there's a peer group organization called Teen Line, which is affiliated with Cedars-Sinai Medical Center. This is a peer-staffed, professionally supervised telephone help line open seven nights a week. Teen volunteers answer more than 10,000 calls a year about sexual abuse, serious depression, drug addiction, AIDS, pregnancy, and other urgent problems that affect young people today. Kids can call (800) TLC-TEEN (852-8336) with any issue and receive direction and resource information that can help them.

Many large metropolitan areas have hot lines, help lines, and support groups for gay teens. One such support group, Out Youth, is based in Austin. Out Youth provides support services for youths aged 13 to 22, and in 1999 it served 400 gay, lesbian, transgendered, and questioning young people. The mission statement on its Web site, outyouth.org, says the group provides support, advocacy, outreach, and general community education.

Project 10 is another program based in Los Angeles. Founded by Virginia Uribe in the mid '80s and now car-

ried on by Gayle Rolf, this is a counseling program established in about 40 of the city's middle and high schools
that offers trained facilitators to meet with gay young
people who need a safe place to come together. The kids
discuss their problems and get the support they need to
stand up to the bigotry and harassment they confront on
a daily basis. As outrageous as it sounds, some of the
boys who have been gay-bashed in their previous schools
were told by administrators that they wouldn't get beat-
en up if they didn't act like such sissies.

Project 10 offers counselor training and workshops for
teachers. While facilitators don't have programs in ele-
mentary schools, they do receive calls from principals
and offer help on an as needed basis to boys and girls
who are being harassed.

Project 10 also has an outreach program, paid for by
private donations, that provides help to private schools
and gives proms for gay boys and girls.

Virginia told me that three or four other cities in
California, along with Cambridge, Mass., have instituted
programs like Project 10 in their schools. She doesn't
know of any other school systems that have such broad-
based programs to protect students and combat homophobia, but Project 10 receives phone calls all the time
from people asking for information about the program.

In an enlightened effort to make a difference, the Los

Angeles Unified School District also offers several alter-
natives to standard high schools. The EAGLES Center
(Emphasizing Adolescent Gay/Lesbian Education
Services) is a small facility designed for only about 30
students. The school offers marginalized kids—cross-
dressers, students with AIDS, kids who have been so
harassed they were unable to stay in their schools—a last
chance to get an education. Were it not for this school
and Jerry Battey, the principal who organized it, many of
these kids would be out on the street.

The OASIS school (Out Adolescents Staying in
School) is another alternative program for extremely
troubled kids in Southern California, with one program
in West Hollywood and another in Long Beach. Joe
Salvemini runs the West Hollywood school, and Sandra
Miller the Long Beach facility. Joe told me that as a general rule, OASIS is for ninth through 12th grades, but in
extreme cases of harassment and gay bashing, it has
taken seventh and eighth graders. It has also taken kids
who have been out for several years and who quit school
rather than face daily harassment. They somehow learn
about OASIS and are happy to be able to come back and
finish their education.

In New York City the Harvey Milk School was founded in 1984 to serve a similar at-risk gay and lesbian
school population. But Joe Salvemini told me that Los

Angeles and New York City are the only two school dis-
tricts in the United States that have programs like these.
This is a very sad state of affairs because, without question, these programs are needed in cities throughout the
country.

In the absence of alternative schools like EAGLES
Center, the Harvey Milk School, and OASIS, sensitivity
training for educators across the country is critically
needed. Even if the kids don't have a school they can
attend where they feel safe and where they are valued,
teacher training to support these kids would at least be a
step in the right direction.

Misunderstandings

Beyond special schools and special programs, we must
ultimately ask ourselves what is being done to help gay
teens in our own community and what kinds of efforts
are being made to make them feel a more integrated part
of society. More than 700 high schools in this country
have gay support groups or gay-straight alliances. But
most schools and school boards refuse to allow the for-
mation of these clubs. The supposedly intelligent leaders
raise issues such as kids bring "recruited" by homosexuals and influenced by their "deviant lifestyle choice."

For all the publicity generated these days about tolerance and understanding, there is a widespread misunderstanding about the purpose of these clubs. *The Los Angeles Times* publishes a weekly question-and-answer column for teens where they may voice their feelings and opinions on a designated subject. Recently the question for the kids was, "Should Gay Clubs Meet on Campus?" One sweet-faced young Korean girl said, "Public schools shouldn't have gay clubs because these clubs send out a message to people that's it's OK to be gay.... I would ask them what the purpose of their club is, and then I would tell them to form their club outside of school because other students might feel uncomfortable." It was perfectly logical to this girl for her Korean club—an organization that, among other things, raises money for the Korean community—to meet on campus. But she saw no reason at all to allow gay students the same privilege. Perhaps this young woman's school—along with all of our schools—should emphasize the importance of the First Amendment and how it applies to our everyday lives.

In an ideal world self-acceptance leads to general acceptance. And general acceptance allows everyone—gay and straight—to be more comfortable with who they are. Obviously, there's still a lot of work to be done. It's time for parents, teachers, and politicians to come together and make every effort to educate kids about the civil rights—as well as the personal rights—of all people before their prejudices become carved in stone. And before more lives become jeopardized.

Fitting In

In Ellen's East Texas high school, the kids didn't think much about civil rights. Their minds were occupied with teenage concerns. Most girls were cheerleaders, in the band, or in the pep squad. Ellen was one of the exceptions. She wasn't interested in any of those things. She liked attending school football games, but on her own terms—which meant going to visit and chat with everyone. Perhaps her willingness and ability to walk her own path when she was a teenager bolstered her courage later in her life when the time came to declare who she was.

Most kids, however, will do anything to fit in, to be approved of by their family and to be liked by their friends. They'll go to any length not to be called "faggot" or "homo" or "dyke." In a February 2000 *Frontline* story, "The Assault on Gay America," Michael S. Kimmel, professor of sociology at State University of New York, Stony Brook, said that in order for boys to be considered masculine, they "must relentlessly repudiate the feminine." It seems to me that this entails killing off a part of themselves that is invaluable.

Because most gay boys and girls don't want to walk the gauntlet of prejudice every day when they go to school, they learn how to blend in. They learn how to fake it. Their goal is to act appropriately masculine or feminine so no one will suspect them of...you know (wink wink)...tendencies. They learn how to dress like other kids. They learn how to talk about who of the opposite sex is cute and who is not, and how to behave on dates. They learn how not to wince when the track coach calls the slowest boy in the relay race a pansy. And they learn how to laugh at fag jokes. These tricks are all part and parcel of the heterosexual hop, a dance learned for the sake of fitting in and mastered for the sake of survival.

Lots of gay kids date members of the opposite sex, especially when they're in high school. After all, it's the perfect cover. I've heard the stories. Lots of them. "I have always accepted the fact I am gay," one young man told me. "I never really hated myself, only the fact I couldn't let people know who I am. I was not 'out' in school. I dated a girl for a little while in high school. We just went to a movie or out to dinner. I liked her as a friend but nothing else. I was uncomfortable even holding hands with her."

And a young woman wrote to me saying, "In high school, I dated the guys that my friends thought I should date. But those 'dates' were groups of us going out to movies, or basketball games and dinner. They weren't 'real dates.'"

I'm glad that Ellen, and those like her who come to an understanding of their sexual orientation a bit later, was spared that kind of teenage turmoil in high school—the years when boys and girls can be especially cruel. These years are difficult enough without sexual confusion making them worse.

I hear the occasional story about a girl taking a girl or a boy taking a boy to the high school prom. The principal objects. School board members throw up their arms in horror. And most of the students shrug and say it's OK with them. But the gutsy kids who are willing to fight their battles on the public turf of proms and sports teams are unusual. Even with all the progress we have made, with all the gay kids who come out, scores of other gay kids still choose to don the camouflage of their presumed orientation. And they pay a painful price for doing so.

As a gay man who had once been married told me, "It takes a lot of energy to be someone you're not."

Just last month I watched the opening festivities of the Super Bowl and got more caught up in it than I thought I would. I couldn't sit still while Tina Turner was singing "Proud Mary." Her energy was contagious. As I watched her I thought, *Sixty years old—you go, girl!*

When Faith Hill sang our national anthem, my emotions went from joy to sadness. As she sang, a group of hearing impaired young people signed the words. They were so beautiful, and as the camera lingered on each fresh face, I wondered how many of these boys and girls would grow up to be gay. And I asked myself if these words of freedom would still apply to them. Or would they too have to join the fight for their equal rights?

I thought of this because looking at them reminded me of the young deaf man I met at the San Francisco gay pride parade, where I was privileged to march with Mayor Willic Brown. A young man named Johnny and I were both wearing Human Rights Campaign caps. I pointed that out to him, and we signed "I love you" to each other. Johnny was with a crowd behind a fence, and I went over and talked to him. I was humbled by how grateful he was. He thanked me for being "Mom," saying his mom and dad had died but they had always been accepting and loving toward him.

This young man very possibly faces discrimination because of his profound hearing loss—and even more because he is gay. Discrimination is evil, for whatever reason. Sadly, Johnny would know.

Fitting Where?

Some kids caught in the throes of adolescent angst aren't quite sure what their orientation is. They find

Dr. Jim Gordon

*San Diego, 1999. My fifth time as grand marshal of a gay pride parade,
giving the sign-language "I love you" sign*

themselves attracted to kids of the same sex, but they're
unable to interpret their feelings and translate them into
some kind of personal insight or self-affirmation. Theirs
is a battle waged in silence and confusion. Often they just
have to wait it out, afraid to confess to their family and
scared to confide in their friends. They hang on until they
cannot contain their truth any longer. And then they
choose the person they trust the most to tell their story to.

Ellen was 20 years old when we took our long walk and
she told me she was a lesbian. In high school she dated
and had several boyfriends—one even gave her a "promise ring" with a tiny diamond chip in it. But on this life-

changing walk she and I took, Ellen told me about that good friend in her senior year who was more than just a friend. This close relationship, she said, was the first stirring of her long-denied sexual orientation.

Whenever boys and girls or men and women realize they are gay, it takes them a while to get used to the idea. And so it was with Ellen. She dated one or two more young men before she was certain that being a lesbian was indeed part of her real self.

I thank God that Ellen and I have always had a close relationship because if ever she needed love and support, she needed it then. Her news that she was gay shook me to the core. I was not prepared to hear this. I'm sure there were signs that could have tipped me off to her homosexuality, had I only been aware enough to pick up on them. But it was a different era then, and I was not as educated or informed as I am now. In regard to homosexuality, no one was.

In spite of the mutual pain we experienced at first, our close relationship has held us together through good times and bad. Ellen understood that just as she needed time to become comfortable with who she was, I needed time to find my own comfort level. Even though I understood what she had told me, I was suddenly forced to revise and refocus all the hopes and dreams I had for her. My visions of her walking down the aisle and someday having children dissolved as abruptly and unexpectedly as any dream does when we awaken to the cold light of day.

Happily, 22 years later, gay and lesbian couples having or adopting children is a reality—and dialogue about same-sex marriage has begun. It's heated, and opposition is strong, but it's a start.

Ellen's revelation that she is gay was shocking—certainly to me and perhaps even to her. This was, after all, the first time she had made her orientation official. The knowledge of who she was and the ability to embrace her identity with family and friends were the first and most important steps she took on the road to personal freedom and honest expression.

Denial vs. Faking

Taking this giant step toward personal freedom requires a level of courage usually acquired bit by bit. Some people find the task daunting and—at least for part of their lives—spend their time denying their orientation or faking heterosexuality.

Denial is different from faking it. Faking it means you know who you are but don't act like who you are. You are not telling others. Denial means you are not telling yourself. You are confused about who you are, and you don't want to deal with the ambivalence. Kids in denial might think they have a little problem, but they figure if they ignore it long enough, it will go away.

Andrew Tobias writes about his denial with heartbreaking detail in his books, *The Best Little Boy in the World* and *The Best Little Boy in the World Grows Up*. He wrote his first book under a pseudonym, as John Reid, in 1973. In 1998 it was reissued under his own name. Tobias was indeed the best little boy in the world—or one of them. His life story is memorable, and his achievements are impressive—all the way through Harvard University and Harvard Business School. During this entire time that he was living a "straight" life, he was aware of—and denying—his homosexuality. He tells of his long and painful journey, and of finally coming to terms with his sexual orientation, with great honesty and humor.

Just like Andrew Tobias, most young people are determined to live up to the expectations of their parents and to live down the suspicions of their friends. They do everything they can to please everyone they can. One young woman told me she did all the things her parents expected of her, including becoming a doctor. The only thing she couldn't do was not be gay. And so her mother and father rejected her.

Often kids are afraid of their family, of what their parents might do if they learn their child is gay. These young people are afraid of being punished or thrown out of the house, of being isolated or disowned. If the kids come from a strong religious background, they can probably gauge just how disruptive their news is going to be. And often the prognosis is not good. So they continue to pretend to be something and someone they are not, even when reality is staring them right in the eyes and telling them the painful truth.

As many of these kids grow older, they bury their heads deeper and deeper in the sands of sexual-identity denial. In a way, the children in denial are the ones who suffer most because the effort it takes to deny who you are can sap all your physical and emotional energy—leaving little emotional strength for dealing with the rest of life.

Often the entire family is in denial. They play peek-a-boo with themselves and with others, behaving like babies who think that if they cover their eyes, whatever is in front of them will disappear. It's as if there is an unspoken conspiracy not to talk about what might be obvious to everyone involved. Eventually these family members learn the hard way that just because they refuse to talk about the elephant in the living room, it doesn't mean it isn't there.

Embracing the Truth

On the flip side of denial are those sensitive and perceptive parents who recognize what is going on in their child's life and do their best to support him or her.

"I think I knew my daughter was gay before she did," a woman wrote me recently. "All through high school and college she would tell me about incredible women writers that she was reading. And so when she finally came to me and said she was gay, I was prepared. In fact, I already knew."

A 31-year-old woman told me that when she broke the news to her parents, her mother said, "It's OK, honey, I've known for years." But her dad didn't know. "I wanted to wait for you," her mom said, "and I'm happy that you finally came to me and told me."

Waiting to be told worked well in this family, but not in the case of the teenage boy who committed suicide rather than tell his family he was gay. His parents knew about his homosexuality but never said one word about it. Their silence erased his identity. Their lack of open support negated his existence.

Chapter Five

To Be or Not to Be

Courage is as often the outcome of despair as of hope;
in the one case we have nothing to lose, in the other
everything to gain.

—Diane de Poitiers

Leaving Home

By their late teens and early 20s, most kids have a clear picture of whether they are gay or straight. Young men and women often see leaving home as an opportunity to begin to come out.

This was an extremely difficult time for Ellen. She was

on the road, just beginning her career in comedy.

Not long ago Ellen and I talked about that period in her life. "I told some comedians I was gay if I thought I could trust them," Ellen said. "This was the hardest time for me. I was either the opening or middle act, performing with men—and fag jokes were in everyone's act."

Building a career *and* keeping a secret extracted its emotional toll. Ellen said that when she began taking questions from the audience at the end of her act, she was always scared that someone in the audience would say, "You're gay, aren't you?"

It's one thing to come out to your family and friends. It's another to come out to the world. When you're still grappling with your fairly recent self-discovery, stepping out of the closet and closing the door behind you is terrifying, especially if you're a public figure.

Declaration of Independence

If a young person is fortunate enough to go to college— better yet, to go away to college—he or she can usually find others who are like-minded. Often, this is the first time in their lives that gay men and women can actually talk to someone about their orientation. Furthermore, most colleges today—unless they have a strict religious character— have some sort of gay and lesbian organization on campus.

This is the point in many kids' lives at which they can finally explore their sexuality. After having to hide and pretend all their lives, they are free for the first time to be who they are.

Sometimes it is easier for young adults to come out to friends and acquaintances before they come out to their family. Certainly many of Ellen's friends knew she was gay before she told me and then the rest of the family. Our children depend on the less judgmental thinking that often goes hand in hand with youth. Furthermore, if the kids are truly frightened of their parents' reactions, they know there's a good chance they could be cut off both emotionally *and* financially. Many kids aren't willing to take this risk, especially with college tuition rocketing into the stratosphere.

I've heard several stories about parents who threaten to stop their son's or daughter's financial support if the child reveals he or she is gay. This fear has stopped many a disclosure—at least until the college degree is in hand.

As a consequence of the fear of a family explosion, many young people go through college putting on acts worthy of an Academy Award. I heard about a man named Caleb who went out with girls all through high school. He was handsome, popular, and personable and had no trouble getting dates. The kids seemed to accept the fact that Caleb didn't want to get involved in a serious relationship.

In college his social situation became a bit more awkward. He was certain he was gay, but he didn't act on those feelings. There was too much family baggage to deal with if he were to come out. Maintaining his cover became a challenge, especially since sex seemed to be part of the dating package by the time he was approaching 20. Caleb was still popular. In fact, he was president of his fraternity at the state university. The only problem was how to maintain his facade when he went out with girls. Caleb hit on the perfect solution: He met and became involved with a devout Catholic girl who didn't believe in sex before marriage. They dated through most of his college years until his overwhelming guilt about leading this girl on caused him to end the relationship.

It wasn't until Caleb left college and got a job in Chicago that he had his first homosexual affair.

There are countless reasons why people don't come out. That said, most gays and lesbians find enormous relief when they finally find the courage to declare themselves. In fact, I haven't spoken to one person who regrets taking that daring step into the light. As one young man told me, "I have very few regrets about school except that I think I should have been courageous enough to come out. That would have made it easier to be who I am, and I wouldn't have had to hide my life from everyone. As it is, I have a pretty good job, and I am out to my Mom."

Coming out is a highly personal step to take. Young people can do it only when they feel ready. Or, to put it more bluntly, when they can no longer live under the weight of lies and pretense.

One man I know attended a large and prestigious Catholic university and simply didn't face the fact that he was gay until he had gotten all the way through college and graduated from law school. When he finally came to terms with his homosexuality, he did it with a vengeance. He now works publicly and proudly for acceptance of gay rights in his university as well as in the workplace.

The Hero Quest

Declaring your homosexuality is often a painful journey fraught with obstacles. Anne and Ellen and I all appreciate the work and philosophy of Joseph Campbell. They have the set of videotapes of his conversations with Bill Moyers, and we also have his books.

In *The Hero With a Thousand Faces*, Campbell writes at length of the Hero Quest—that journey from darkness to light that forms the basis for nearly all storytelling, from ancient Greek classics to myths and fairy tales to modern-day novels. The Hero Quest is the bedrock of the universal adventure and the foundation of most self-realized lives.

The dramatic story structure of the Hero Quest follows a loosely defined but universally recognized set of rules. Think of Jonah and the whale, *The Great Gatsby*, or even *The Wizard of Oz*. The heroes of these stories all go through a period of darkness in which they must struggle with real or imagined demons before they can emerge, transformed, into the light.

St. John of the Cross refers to our worst moments—that season in the belly of the whale—as "the dark night of the soul." This is the time in our life when we surrender to the fact that we must go inward in order to be reborn. As painful as this process is, Campbell says, as soon as the hero steps outside the bounds of his or her tradition, it is inevitable that he or she will encounter demons that are simultaneously harbingers of danger and bestowers of magic.

Campbell calls this time of pain and struggle a "life-centering, life-renewing act." And he defines the elements of the Hero Quest with deceiving simplicity.

1) In the beginning, the hero is called to action.
2) An irresistible force impels him to accept.
3) The hero crosses over into the underworld, where he meets a guide who helps him overcome a series of challenges as he tries to obtain the ultimate boon—truth.

4) When the hero achieves the ultimate truth, he is in the greatest danger, both physically and morally. Here he becomes godlike because only he knows the truth.

5) He isn't certain he can leave the underworld.

6) Finally the hero decides to return to the upper world, but he is changed forever and cannot return to where he began.

A few weeks ago I received a letter from a young man named Gregory whose pilgrimage from childhood to adulthood embodies the elements of the Hero Quest and imbues it with uncommon grace. I suspect that most gay men and women can relate to his story— and that most friends and family can respect it.

I'm a 31-year-old male living in a small Kentucky town. I knew I was different from other boys back in third grade because I just didn't play the same way they did. While the boys were playing sports and roughhousing at recess, I was hanging out with the girls because they weren't as "mean-spirited."

In our neighborhood, when my friends were playing basketball and riding bicycles, I was in the backyard organizing carnivals, putting on shows, and play-acting Lost in Space. *I was the only kid who would make costumes, including the robot, out of cardboard and duct tape. I* made super props for everyone—capes, Wonder Woman bracelets—you name it, I could re-create it. I was considered an odd bird in the neighborhood, but damn if I couldn't entertain them all!

By fifth and sixth grade, I was already being called all the usual names, "faggot," "queer," "homo." At that point, I didn't know what they meant (we didn't have cable), but I felt, from their tone, it must not be a "good" thing to be. While my friends who were boys began talking about crushes on this girl or that, I sat waiting for those feelings to hit me. All the while, I was captivated by different men on television or other guys in school. When I learned what "faggot" meant and I knew I felt that way, I retreated into a shell because it wasn't "right."

By high school I was a constant target for bullying and taunting. Hardly a day went by that I wasn't called a derogatory name or pushed into a locker. I was sometimes threatened with being beaten up, and for nothing more than just walking down the hall. I never expressed any indication of my sexuality, hoping to simply blend into the crowd; but it didn't work. I was terrified to walk from class to class. At the mall I would rush from store to store, hoping not to be seen by anyone who might make fun of me. Even at the movie theater, I remember having gum stuck in my hair by someone who leaned in behind me and whispered, "You're a faggot, aren't you?" and (even *worse epithets). I was hated for just being alive.*

In class, when I had to get up before the other students, I remember more than once being called the usual names, and the teachers never did a thing about it. They just acted like nothing was said. No one was reprimanded for what they did, and that made me feel like they had the teachers' approval. I never felt like I could turn to my teachers for guidance or support.

I coped by hiding as much as I could. If I could have turned invisible, I would have. I rented every movie that came out in the mid '80s and holed up in my house on the weekends.

Fortunately, I went to college right out of high school and almost immediately fell in with a good, supportive group of friends. I became more comfortable with myself and began to come out of my shell. It would be years later before I even dared to think about coming out of the closet. But I had met a number of strong, confident gays and lesbians—many of whom became very good friends. They never pushed the subject with me. They let me take my own steps.

When I finally found the courage to come out of the closet, I was met with more support and understanding than I ever imagined. My friends have stood by me; my family and coworkers have stood by me; and for the first time in my life, I feel like I'm truly alive.

This is the journey from darkness to light that most seekers—gay and straight—must take. And, like this young man, it is only at the completion of this quest that they can find their fulfillment. And their redemption.

The Journey Into the World

Often the hero's journey doesn't even begin until children leave home and feel more comfortable with exploring who they are and what they stand for.

Finally school's out. Students graduate and—college degree in hand—become financially independent, responsible, full-fledged adults. If young people haven't been to college, they've most likely been working for several years by this time.

If gays and lesbians haven't come out yet, the early 20s can be the perfect time, especially if they live in or near a large metropolitan area. Most big cities in America have a strong and vibrant gay community. There are gay nightclubs, gay support groups, and gay bookstores and coffee shops—all offering the promise of no longer having to stand alone in a hostile world.

This is the age when many gay men and women have their first serious, meaningful relationships. Naturally, they want to share their happiness with those who mean the most to them. This usually includes their family.

I've written in my previous book about the first girl-friend of Ellen's I ever met. Ellen, however, recently reminded me of an even earlier girlfriend—a young woman our family knew and liked. This was really Ellen's *first* girlfriend. Ellen has also told me about another of her girlfriends, one I unfortunately never met, a woman who was killed in a car accident.

Her friend's death was a tragedy in Ellen's life. At the time, she was living in a damp, dingy basement apartment full of fleas and roaches—and her vibrant young girlfriend was killed. This event eventually led to Ellen's "Phone Call to God" comedy routine—a classic for her. In it she asks God why we have fleas, and God reminds her of all the jobs provided by the flea-collar industry, and on and on. As always, she used humor to cover her depression and to work through a low period in her life.

Looking back on our lives, I'm proud of my family and the way we have supported each other and stuck together. Ellen's friends and girlfriends have always been included in and welcomed to family functions. And I think that speaks well of us. Perhaps that feeling of trust and acceptance was always there. That's something we never really think about until it gets tested.

Although my family has been supportive of Ellen, I know it's not easy for kids to come out to parents who have always assumed their son or daughter would grow up, get married to someone of the opposite sex, and have children. Part of the anxiety that surrounds telling your parents is the fear that they will be angry or upset with you. The other part stems from the knowledge that, no matter how much your mother and father love and support you, the revelation you are about to share with them will likely disappoint and distress them.

Even though your parents may love you dearly, even though they may have suspected, even though they may have caught a glimpse of your sexuality but looked the other way—when you tell them you are gay, they will still be bewildered. But I would urge you to step back a moment and take a deep breath. Bewildered does not mean your parents do not love you. Bewildered does not mean they do not care. It simply means they might need some time to get used to the idea.

As a mother, I can guarantee you that once the initial shock has passed, given enough time, loving parents will eventually embrace who you are.

Stage Fright

If the thought of coming out to your family sends you into fits of fear and dread, try to structure the circumstances so that you will be as comfortable as possible. As painful and anxiety-ridden as the pending revelation might be, most people opt to break their news face to face. But one young woman told me that she found the courage to tell her parents only when she was two states away. Distance created the safety she needed to be true to herself. If you need to make a telephone call in order to confront the truth, then by all means pick up the phone and begin this honest dialogue.

Truth or Consequences

Not long ago I asked my therapist friend Dr. Dina Bachelor Evan about the ramifications of coming out and the consequences of hiding. This is what she wrote.

I never came out. I came home. Before I knew I was a lesbian, I lived in a straight world as a visitor, never knowing why I didn't fit in and trying everything I knew to feel at home. Four children and a whole lifetime later, I discovered I was a lesbian in straight lady's clothing. Finally, in the midst of an acquiescing sigh, I understood. I felt so much joy that I could hardly contain myself. The kind of joy you feel when you find the perfect new outfit. The one that makes you feel ten pounds lighter and irresistibly attractive. I bubbled. I blissed. I relished. I rejoiced. Little did I know what this revelation would require!

There are certain things in life that act as spiritual

wake-up calls. The car that nearly misses you as you step off the curb. The person whose eyes meet yours across the room in the silent recognition that you are, without ever having met, inextricably entwined. The flight you missed that crashes, the first time you experience prejudice, and discovering you are gay or lesbian and that most of the world will hate you for it.

If you are conscious, being gay or lesbian is the fire that demands that you be who you are. It provides you with choices—Lie? Tell the truth? Hide? Stand up? Give up? Fight back?—the consequences of which serve to profoundly either enhance or diminish your level of character and authenticity.

When you are straight, no one knows at first glance whether or not you have integrity or personal pride. You are not confronted in the same way with these questions. But once you realize you are gay or lesbian, every question about your level of emotional courage is instantly in your face. It hovers in the air between you and your beloved as you step out the front door of your home and must decide, "Do I keep holding her hand or let it go?" It goes with you to work and creeps into your awareness when an associate asks about getting together for dinner and expresses a wish to meet your husband. It hangs on the telephone line when your family wants to know who you are dating, whether it is serious, and "when can we meet him?"

Come Out, Come Out, Wherever You Are

When we come out to friends and coworkers, there isn't nearly as much at stake as when we come out to our family.

This was true for Ellen. And this is why she cried when she told me she was gay. I can imagine her terror, not knowing how I would react. She'd heard the stories. She was about to tell me something that has caused other parents to reject their children, to throw them out of the house and never speak to them again. For all she knew, her news might bring all our years of closeness to an abrupt halt.

I don't think my initial response was the wisest and most supportive that I could have offered. But it wasn't the worst response either. Even though I was stunned by what I was hearing, I knew that nothing was going to come between us—which is why I hugged her and tried to calm her fears.

Ellen gave me the time I needed to come to terms with this staggering news and to become educated about a subject that I never in a million years thought would concern me.

Initially, Ellen's father and his wife, Virginia, had an unfortunate reaction to her news. They asked her to leave their house so Virginia's small children wouldn't be "influenced." This was ignorance in action, and they have long since expressed their regrets about this.

Today, our extended family consists of devout Catholics, Episcopalians, Presbyterians, and more, and no one has shunned Ellen or acted distant in any way. Knowing these wonderful people as I do, I can't say that I'm surprised.

Fantasyland

We all want the love and approval of our parents. We need their validation to become a whole human being. And because of that need, we never tire of hearing them say, "I'm proud of you." When parents base their love and approval on a condition that can't be met, the results can be devastating.

Part of the problem, I think, is that we grow up in ignorance, unaware of people all around us who are gay. In an effort to shed a new light on this notion, let me suggest that we all know someone who is left-handed. Lefties make up about 10% of the population, roughly the same percentage as gay people. And yet millions of Americans say they don't know anyone who is gay. Unless those people who claim ignorance are living in a gated community called Fantasyland, they are most likely mistaken.

Not long ago I heard a wonderful story about an anonymous person in Nashville who funded a prominent billboard that said SOMEONE YOU KNOW AND LOVE IS GAY. A simple, factual message. The workman who put up the sign defaced it the same day.

Needless to say, this act of vandalism got masses of publicity. A TV station interviewed the workman and edited the piece to make him sound sympathetic to gay issues. This got him in trouble with his fundamentalist church. This too was news. When all was said and done, the billboard company fixed the sign and kept it up one month past the contract date. They obviously thought the First Amendment was more important than one man's opinion.

The Rejection Collection

Not everyone lives in a city where a billboard message supports them. And not everyone has the privilege of coming out of the closet without being punished. Recently I heard about a Hispanic man whose parents have rejected him for being gay. When he calls home to try to talk to his mother, she says, "You have the wrong number," and hangs up.

As a human being, I am disgusted. As a mother, I am horrified. That this woman would rather embrace outdated ideas and endorse hateful behavior than have a loving relationship with her son is unfathomable to me. Hers is an extreme reaction but, unfortunately, one that no longer shocks me. I've heard hundreds of stories ranging from total rejection to complete acceptance—and all degrees in between. And I am no longer surprised at what parents are capable of, both the good and the bad.

A woman I spoke to recently told me that 15 years ago she came out to her mother. Her mother then told her daughter not to tell her father. Today, 15 years later, the secret still lingers—only the mother knows. And, needless to say, the resentment still festers.

In the February 29, 2000, issue of *The Advocate*, psychotherapist Betty Berzon addresses this issue with sensitivity and wisdom. "Please do not become a powerless kid with no voice and no presence," she says. "Make the choice to declare who you are and challenge the enlightenment and humanity of your family member.

"Many parents react to the revelation that an offspring is gay or lesbian by sexualizing the news. And just as most children don't want to think of their parents as sexual beings, most parents don't want to think of their children, even as adults, as sexual beings. So a revelation about being gay becomes uncomfortable—because homosexuality is all about sex, isn't it? Of course it's not, and that is a major reason to keep talking about your gay life in all its complexities. You can't just stop with coming out and really be understood. That is barely the beginning."

My Own Family Miracle

I am witness to the fact that persistence in the face of parental rejection can have a happy ending. I'm delighted to tell you here that after being rejected for three years, my other "daughter," Anne Heche, has reestablished communications with her mother. Anne has spoken honestly, as she always does, of her family's rejection of her. And I have written of the sadness we all experienced because Anne's family could not seem to accept her relationship with Ellen.

Just before Christmas Anne called her mother again. "This time with no expectations," she said. "I came to understand," Anne told me, "that I was rejecting my mother for her beliefs in the same manner that she was rejecting me for my beliefs. It took me two and a half years to realize that I was being as shut down as I thought she was being.... I finally came to a place where I was able to understand and embrace our differences and love her for them. Potentially this would heal me and open up the possibility of communication without expectation of the result. Because I was able to open my heart

The Los Angeles premiere of HBO's If These Walls Could Talk 2 was made extra joyous because Anne's mother, Nancy, and sister, Abigail, were there to share it with us.

to that, it allowed her to open her heart to me."

Anne continued in her ever-so-articulate way, "Everybody has the right to feel what he or she feels, but if one is in judgment—if one does not have a compassionate heart—there's no chance of ever coming to understanding. I gave my mother a space and a place. We agreed to love each other—in spite of our differences."

Since the time Anne made that "no expectations" phone call, she has had many conversations with her family, and they are all happily on the road to healing. A few weeks ago Anne's mother sent Ellen a birthday gift. We hope to all get together soon, and we are delighted to welcome Anne's family into our hearts and homes.

Never give up!

One Woman's Story

As happy as Anne's story is turning out to be, even when they persist in their efforts at reconciliation, not all families can change a bad ending into a good one. Sometimes not even the miracle of birth is powerful enough to reconcile people with closed minds and shriveled spirits—especially when religion is involved. My friend Dr. Dina Bachelor Evan told me the following story about her own family and what happened with her two daughters when she came out.

The depth of my new discovery first rippled through me when one of my daughters asked, "How can you be a lesbian? You're not with anyone."

And I answered, "How can you be straight? Neither are you." It was at that point that both she and I understood the issue of sexuality and sexual orientation was not about choice. She was the only one with a choice, and she chose to love me anyway.

On the other hand, my oldest daughter, a Jehovah's Witness, called to tell me she wanted me to be at the birth of her firstborn child. Because of her religion's restrictions, she had chosen to separate herself from the rest of the family. I hadn't seen her for several years, so I was elated to hear her voice. I remember that call as if it happened yesterday, although it was 15 years ago. "I want you to be at the birth," she said. "But of course you won't be able to spend time with the child after it's born. You know...because of your lifestyle."

My heart dropped to the floor. After I found the strength to speak again, I said, "I'm sorry, honey; I can't bond with this child and then have it leave my life like you did. I love you, but I can't be there." I never spoke with my daughter again. I've never held any of her children. It is as if my firstborn died the day of that call. To this day it is her choice not to have me in her life. "You know...because of your lifestyle."

For me, being a lesbian is a spiritual assignment that has to do with integrity, authenticity, compassion, and love. Being a woman who loves women is the fire in my spiritual process, the purifier of my soul. If I am to be authentic, that part of who I am must be honored. It is not a choice. I cannot extricate my love for women from who I am spiritually any more than I can extricate my love for Spirit from who I am. They are magically interwoven to create the tapestry of my soul. Each time I stand up for either I am somehow made whole, more powerful, more real. Each time I stand up, I make the statement that being a lesbian is not about who I love, it's about how I love. Deeply, powerfully, and from my soul with great pride.

Shhh

Not telling other family members or close friends about your sexual orientation or the orientation of your child perpetuates the very sense of shame and pretense that the gay person is trying to overcome. Not long ago, the mother of a gay daughter asked me how to deal with this problem. "There are certain people I know I can tell, but there are others that I'm not sure of," she said. "What do I say when people ask, 'So how's Sue? Any boyfriends yet? Dating anyone special? Will we see her walking down the aisle any time soon?'"

Ideally, this mother should answer the second question with, "No, Sue is gay, but we like all of her friends very much. They're fine young women—just like Sue." To question number three: "Yes. Sue is gay and has been in a relationship for five years now. We love her partner like she's another daughter. We feel very lucky." And to question number four, this woman should be able to answer, "I hope so. Sue is in a committed relationship.

We hope she and her life partner will someday have the right to legally marry."

I've been in both situations and at both extremes—from having to keep our family secret to being open and honest and feeling free to say, "Yep, she's gay." Believe me, open and honest is better. Ellen wasn't the only one liberated by the truth. I was too.

I realize our situation is different from the average private citizen's. At the beginning of her career, Ellen didn't feel free to be honest about this most basic part of her being. So, of course, the family followed her lead. It wasn't my place to divulge her secret. But secrets are wearing. When Ellen could no longer live with the weight of that burden, she decided to be honest no matter the consequences. Once her secret was revealed, the weight was lifted—from her and from all of us.

But the reality of coming out is rarely so cut-and-dried. I can't advise parents to tell someone about their child's sexuality if that someone will react in a contemptible way. But I can advise parents to be as honest as they can, whenever and however they can—even if they suspect the situation is marginal. Think about it: Do you really want to be friends with someone who would denigrate or reject your child merely because he or she is gay?

The Power of Power

I often wonder about gay people who are well-known in the film industry or in other high-powered, high-profile jobs. Gay people are everywhere, in greater numbers and in more prominent positions than most people imagine. On the one hand, I understand why they remain in the closet. If they reveal the truth, their jobs, their income, and their future work could be put in jeopardy. Certainly Ellen knew full well that she was gambling with her career when she came out in 1997. But she was willing to risk success for the privilege of finally living her life honestly and proudly.

She was a pioneer in taking this bold step. There were no landmarks for her to follow, no one who did it before that she could look to and say, "Uh-oh, they did that wrong. I'd better try it this way." She was a first and has gone on record saying she has no regrets and would do it all again, despite losing her beloved TV show.

Anne too has paid a price for her unflinching honesty. Like Ellen, she had never known discrimination until she acknowledged she is a lesbian. She had just risen to "star" status. Her career was skyrocketing. Suddenly roles were not offered and auditions were not opened to her. Anne is a gifted actress, and the thought of her being passed over because of her relationship with Ellen was unbearable. After all, her profession is called *acting*. Why should Anne's private life interrupt or distract from her proven acting skills? Sure, it was causing a stir. What was she supposed to do? Keep it a secret? Let's face it, a relationship between Anne and Ellen would be almost impossible to hide. Neither one was willing to even try.

But with all the difficulties they encountered, their story has a happy ending. Ellen has said all she ever wanted to do was entertain people, to make them laugh. She's doing that again, in several different venues. Happily, Anne is writing and directing—in addition to her acting. Talent wins out. And in these cases, so does courage.

Since Anne and Ellen opened the door, the atmosphere in Hollywood is more receptive to gay men and lesbians than it has ever been. What a powerful message it would be if all the gay people in Hollywood—actors, producers, directors—were to step out of the closet and declare themselves. I often wonder why more people don't do it. Ellen did it. After an initial reversal of fortune, her career is back on track. Anne did it. And now she has several movies lined up. Rupert Everett did it. His star status is greater than ever. Some of the most famous closeted gay actors, singers, and entertainers I know have enough money to last ten lifetimes. They don't need the work. They don't need the fame. And they don't need the influence that power brings them.

Tyler St. Mark, a writer-producer I've met, wrote an article for *The Los Angeles Times* on this very subject. Since he is gay, his words carried extra weight. His arguments for coming out were powerful, and he ended his article by saying:

It is a paradox that straight people prefer to see homosexuals flamboyant and outrageous on the screen but silent and conservative in real life. It is a greater paradox that gay people are quick to spot homophobia in others but fail to see their own self-oppression.

Gay people permeate our industry, from studio heads and production executives to camera operators and talent agents. Responsibility begins not with the activist and media watchdog, but with each and every gay person in the biz who is in a position to advance and enhance positive and accurate gay portrayals in film.

You know who you are. Time to move from the back of the pack and run out in front.

If everyone who is gay or lesbian would just say so, the response would be overwhelming. With so many productive, creative—and, yes, famous—people in every corner of this country saying, "Yep, I'm gay," the religious right would have to manufacture a new bandwagon to jump on. And the rest of the world could breathe a sigh of relief.

If Not Now, When?

In my experience, once a family heads down the road of secrecy, what once was a source of pride can turn into a burden of shame. After finally finding the courage to come out, everything possible should be done to validate this experience—including telling those whom others think should not be told.

In her acclaimed book of essays, *A Chorus of Stones*, Susan Griffin talks about the monumental and disastrous consequences of one part of a family keeping secrets from the other—and how that secret is passed from one generation to the next. Denial, turning our back on the truth, often hinges on a perceived source of shame. And Griffin brilliantly tells the story of what happens when the secret corrodes. And explodes.

In her essay she likens her father to a stone, refusing to face the reality that confronted him. Yet even the stone, she reminds us, is etched by the wind and the rain. "Perhaps we are like stones," Griffin says, "our own history and the history of the world embedded in us, we hold a sorrow deep within and cannot weep until that history is sung."

Although an entire family can deny the existence of a gay parent or son or daughter, not one member of that family can fail to be affected by this fact. Whether we acknowledge or deny it, truth will make its mark. It's up to us to choose whether we wear this mark as a scar of secrecy or a badge of honor.

Standing in the Light

Needless to say, the news of your own or your child's sexual orientation doesn't have to be trumpeted from the treetops. It might just be a case of not denying the truth if Uncle Milton or Aunt Doris asks for it. However, if you have a friend or family member who would create more trouble than the truth is worth, then keeping the secret could possibly be justified. This said, I would urge you to take a deep breath and stand in the light whenever and however you can. No one I've ever talked to has regretted taking this step. The only stories of regret I have heard are about waiting so long to come out.

As more and more parents are able to answer the questions of friends and family in a straightforward, honest way, the subject of homosexuality is bound to lose its mystery and myth. This is why PFLAG is so important.

In "Ask Betty," my advice column on PlanetOut.com, I

sometimes feel like a broken record. But so many questions involve how to tell parents or how to help parents become more accepting. And, in every case, PFLAG is the answer. I advise gay people to go to the meetings for ideas on the best ways to tell their parents and what to expect when they do. And I certainly advise parents to go, to join, and to become active members. I've had feedback from one mother who did just that. Prior to this she had accepted that her daughter is a lesbian but acted as though she had a shameful secret. Now she's active in PFLAG and speaking out for equal rights for gays and lesbians.

My favorite PFLAG story is about the wonderful, inspiring couple I met in Florida—both active members in the organization. They have several children and five grandchildren, none of whom are gay. They go to the meetings because they just want to help end the ignorance and the hatred that ignorance breeds.

Stranger in a Strange Land

In *Love, Ellen* I told the story of a 76-year-old lesbian who wrote to Ellen and said she never thought she'd see an openly gay lead on a TV show—and a show done with such "poignancy, taste, and humor." Later Ellen joked in a speech, "And me being new to all this, I didn't know

Anne Heche

My dear friend Harriet Perl, the "76-year-old lesbian," and me

there were 76-year-old lesbians."

That 76-year-old lesbian is now 79 and jokes about being "frozen in time." Harriet has since become a good friend of mine. She knows from her own experience about keeping secrets. Harriet was a teacher for many years. After she retired and finally came out, she talked to people with whom she had taught. They said they realized she was gay, but no one had dared say a word about it.

"I envied Ellen for being able to say to you, 'Mom, I'm gay,' and for your loving response," Harriet told me. "By the time I knew I was gay, I didn't even know there was a word for what I felt. As far as I knew, I was absolutely alone in the world. Even later, when I learned there were others like me, finding them was misery and life was a matter of guarding my secret. My parents would never have accepted my sexuality—if they had even understood what I was talking about. It was a different world back in the 1930s and '40s."

Harriet continued, "Growing older isn't easy in our youth-worshiping culture. In fact, one of the things I wish Ellen could have done before ABC closed her off was to address the whole issue of older lesbians—or just plain older women, regardless of sexual orientation. You and Ellen and Anne have addressed yourselves generously to the plight of the young who are struggling with their sexuality and their families. But I was hoping you would acknowledge the lives of the older women who got no help from anywhere as they came out to themselves, never mind to the world."

Other older lesbians I've heard about have lived most of their lives as heterosexuals. They didn't even acknowledge their sexual orientation until they were older.

One 87-year-old woman told me, "My awareness did not occur until I was 56. Not until I'd married three times and had a child did I realize I was different from the women in the heterosexual world."

Not long ago I heard about a woman who was in a 42-year relationship with another woman and no one knew—not family and not friends. She finally came out at age 70.

And then there are the two men who have been in a loving relationship for 57 years—and each man has family members who have never met their relative's partner. What a loss, not only for the men but for the families too.

Let's Pretend

All these stories remind me of when I was in high school and my sister, Helen, was teaching at Louisiana State University. She had a good friend named Marietta who lived with another woman. The two were always together. Sometimes they would drive Helen home for weekends and pick her up to go back to school. Years later, it occurred to Helen and me that Marietta and her friend were gay—that they were a couple. They lived together and grew old together.

In those days their relationship could never have been acknowledged and validated. They had secrets they couldn't share. They had anniversaries that no one celebrated. They even bought a house together. They did all the things that heterosexual couples are congratulated for. They cared deeply for each other—and yet they spent their lives pretending to be nothing more than roommates. I wonder what this must have done to their spirit. All of this pretense so they, as members of a minority group, could fit unnoticed and untormented into heterosexual society.

Women of my generation know something about pretending and fitting in. Most of us grew up hearing, "Don't do that. What will people think? That's not ladylike. You shouldn't feel that way." The message was clear: Be nice and fit in. Don't be your authentic self. And above all: Don't make waves.

Beyond those basic rules of comportment, the unspoken message was that a woman is nobody without a man. As a woman, your highest purpose in life was to find a good man so you could be a good wife and mother.

After my last marriage ended, I was still buying into that message. I continued to think I should find a good man and be a good wife. It didn't occur to me that not everybody gets to play Cinderella and meet Prince Charming. Fortunately for me, I didn't meet another man to marry. And because of that, for the first time in my life, I've given myself permission to find out who I really am. My freedom is exhilarating, and I am finally being true to myself. After a lifetime of conformity, I've discovered that there is a delicious joy in facing the world just as myself.

Appreciating my newfound freedom made my conversation with a woman just a few weeks ago all the more poignant. Thelma is a dean at a small community college. She and her "friend" have been living together for 31 years. I asked her if her being gay has ever made a difference in her work, in whether she got promoted or in any other area of college life.

"Why should it?" she said. "Nobody knows."

Someone then brought up my work as spokesperson for the Human Rights Campaign's National Coming Out Project.

The same woman said, "Why would you want to make people come out?"

I assured her I don't want to make anyone do anything but that I believe coming out is such a healthy step to take that, through this project with the Human Rights Campaign, I am encouraging everyone who is thinking of being honest about their sexual orientation to do so.

I suppose that if you're 50 or 60 or 70 years old, secrecy has become such an ingrained habit that the thought

Judy G. Rolfe

What a group! Elizabeth Birch (executive director of the Human Rights Campaign), Anne, Ellen, me, Judy and Dennis Shepard, and Vance. The occasion was the October 9, 1999, HRC National Dinner.

of coming out is terrifying. But I often wonder how closeted older gay people would feel if, after all these years, they found the courage to turn to their neighbor and say, "I am gay." My suspicion is that they would experience abject terror. But they would also experience indescribable relief.

Of course, this feels very much like my own scary but ultimately joyous journey toward coming out as a single woman—on my own as my own person without a husband. Terrified at first but supremely happy now.

Still Hiding After All These Years—Our Gay Senior Citizens

The heads of gay and lesbian senior citizens must be spinning over the changes taking place in the lives of gay people today. When older gays and lesbians were growing up, they lived in a land where everyone was heterosexual. Homosexuals didn't exist. Society was viewed through such a skewed lens that anything less than the Cleaver family was dismissed as unthinkable.

A friend of mine named Pamela, who is 60 years old, told me recently that she was raised in an upper class, white neighborhood in Kansas City.

"My parents had a good marriage," she said. "They loved each other, and they loved my sister and me. I just assumed that all the other families I knew were the same way." Pamela laughed when she told me this. "By the time I got out of college, I had heard shocking stories about people I grew up with. People I knew well. One brother and sister I went to school with were 'doing it' in the basement of their home. Two of my friends had fathers who were raging alcoholics. Another man I knew molested his daughter and his niece. And two friends of mine had mothers who molested them. I heard of all these secrets, all these dysfunctional horrors," she added, "but not one word was ever even murmured about the simple fact that anyone in any family was gay. As far as I was concerned, 'gay' didn't exist. As a matter of fact, I didn't even know what a homosexual was until I was a senior in college."

Imagine growing up gay in a world like Pamela's. Imagine the confusion you would experience if you couldn't even put a name to your feelings—much less bring some insight or understanding to them. It's no wonder that there are thousands and thousands of closeted senior citizens living all across America. In their day, coming out would have been tantamount to social suicide. A lady or a gentleman couldn't and wouldn't do such a thing. Their secret has been kept for a lifetime, and now they think it's too late to change. But it isn't.

The Tragic Price of Secrets

Dr. Jim Gordon says that ignoring anyone for being gay makes that person feel like less than a full person. The gay man or woman is still allowed to be a member of the family, but it's a restricted membership. The whole person is denied entry to the clan. Being treated this way can lead to all sorts of tragic behavior by the gay family member, with the extreme being suicide.

John, a friend of mine in Dallas, told me that he tormented himself with "feelings of panic, shame and self-hate for 37 years" until he came out. "Growing up I only knew two people that were gay," he said. "A flamboyant type and an effeminate type. I wasn't like either of them, and I didn't know anybody else who was gay. My parents were very liberal and into human rights, but they made fun of gay people and tried, unsuccessfully, to remove the softer traits from my demeanor. What is so sad is that I had some wonderful role models right in my own family, and they were denied to me."

I love what my friend Dr. Dina Bachelor Evan, who discovered her homosexuality later in life, has to say about secrets and the toll they take on the spirit:

The very foundation of healthy relationships is communication and honesty. A person cannot have meaningful relationships and hold back the biggest part of who he or she is. Secrets diminish our self-esteem, our sense of being lovable and our level of character. Acting as if being gay or lesbian is something to be hidden or shame-filled about diminishes who we are at a spiritual level. In 16 years of psychotherapy practice, I have only experienced two people whose families actually disowned them once they announced that they were gay or lesbian. Countless others found that although the information was troubling to parents or relatives, they soon were able to focus on the love they felt instead of the difference.

As gay men and lesbians, we have internalized a sense of shame that causes us to feel others will judge us. Unfortunately, society is living on our shame and projects it back to us. We are living in a society that is addicted to sameness. We have the mentality that if we are not the same, something is wrong. And if something is wrong, that means either I am wrong or you are. We tout support for diversity, and yet every minority in this country is under some form of oppression.

The pressure is to conform, get in line, and be the same as the rest of us. Those who do come out, regardless of the cost, have reclaimed a part of themselves and honored it. The cost is great, and yet, as those on this path know, it is more honorable to live being fully who we are—no matter what our color, our heritage, or our gender preference—than to spend a lifetime making ourselves and everyone else comfortable.

Gay and lesbian people who hold back this secret diminish their power in the world and their rightful place in society. This practice of "hiding the secret" begins early, when we discover that we are somehow different than others. We begin to internalize that difference as something bad. We spend lifetimes covering up, so as not to be proven bad. Much in the same way, an alcoholic family covers up the secret as if it were about them instead of the alcoholic.

Shame is not about us. Shame is never something we

naturally feel; it is something projected onto us. If we are doing something wrong, we feel remorse, sadness, regret, but never shame.

Those who hold on to their secret spend inordinate amounts of time covering up pieces and parts of themselves while life passes them by. When parents come to visit, houses are de-lesbianized and made to be "normal." Pictures get hidden. Appearances get changed so that there is no suspicion two men or two women are sleeping in the same bedroom.

The cancer of pretending moves inevitably into our own homes and bedrooms. At the same time we diminish the risk of being found out, we also diminish the importance of our partners. Often to the point of losing the relationship.

We spend hours wondering what it might feel like to be heterosexual, what it is to feel normal. We are visitors in both worlds, caught in the place between called fear. On one side, we cannot be open and gay, and on the other, we cannot be authentically heterosexual. We live "nowhere" until we come out.

Those who are not out often have difficulty maintaining relationships, careers, and school. Many move often, fearing they will be found out and ridiculed. This pattern soon erodes self-esteem and any sense of accomplishment in life.

We have a tendency to judge ourselves harshly. We begin

to believe we have brought the discomfort to our families, rather than that our families have chosen the discomfort, by simply being who we are. We are therefore caught in a no-win situation. If we come out and be who we are, in our own perception and that of others, we are causing pain. If we do not come out, we are killing ourselves. The longer it takes us to come out, the greater the shame we heap upon ourselves for being too weak. This cycle sets up a lifetime of conflict. It deadens our sense of aliveness. It diminishes the joy in our lives and sets us up in a conflict where we can never win.

Chapter Six

And a Little Child Shall Lead Them

Who else speaks for the Family of Man?
—Carl Sandburg

All My Children

Once a gay couple has developed a committed relationship, they may decide that they want to have children. Obviously, this isn't the walk in the parental park that most heterosexual couples take. Gay couples must decide between adoption, surrogacy, or in vitro fertilization. They must also think about whether they are living in a place where their family will be accepted. If not, they might consider moving to a location and a school district where their child will be more comfortable.

While gay and lesbian couples who adopt or have children may be more common these days, it certainly is not a new idea. For instance, I know of two women whose son now has his Ph.D.

Today, because of divorce or loss, millions of men and women are raising children alone. Single women who want to experience the joys of motherhood and have love to give to a child are turning to a friend or to sperm banks to get pregnant. Single men who don't want to be deprived of the joy and privilege of being a parent adopt or father a child.

Single men and women and gay couples often adopt hard-to-place babies and children or unwanted girl babies from China. There are, of course, those who say that these unconventional arrangements aren't families. We've heard their ugly, strident voices. Whenever I encounter them, I tell them that if home is where the heart is, so is family. Even when no children are involved, I wouldn't presume to tell couples like the two women in Maryland who have been together 54 years or the two men in North Carolina who have been together 44 years that they are not a family.

When gay couples decide to have a baby, this is no spur-of-the-moment decision. And it obviously can't just be a happy mistake. Sometimes it takes years to go through sperm donor, surrogacy, or adoption procedures. I know of couples who enter counseling before having or adopting a child in order to make sure they want babies for all the right reasons.

Anne and Ellen often talk about the possibility of having children. They both have big hearts and would love to have a baby. They also have very busy careers and know that any plans for a family need to be put on hold for a few years. For the moment they're content to take pleasure in the company of their friends' children.

Earlier this year, Melissa Etheridge and Julie Cypher—who have two children—announced the identity of their sperm donor. In a high-profile case like this, rumors were flying, with Brad Pitt being the world's fantasy donor of choice. In an article in *Rolling Stone* magazine, Melissa said that because of all the rumors and because she and Julie live their lives openly and honestly, they had finally decided to reveal that the father of their children is musician David Crosby. Comedians had a field day with this information. But when the dust settles and it's yesterday's news, I'm sure Melissa and Julie will feel that going public with the information was the right thing to do.

Anyone who reads the *Rolling Stone* article can't help

but be impressed with the way these two women are living their lives, and can't help but respect the thought and care they give to raising their two children.

I recently found an old journal with notes I made on November 16, 1997. "We (Ellen and I) visited two lesbian friends of El's—a loving couple with a darling nine-month-old girl. There couldn't be a more loving, intelligent, mentally stimulating atmosphere for a baby. (That couple was Julie and Melissa.) Another couple was visiting with their 11-month-old girl. This too was a nontraditional family. Yet here too this baby couldn't be surrounded by more love, support, and caring." (This couple was Kathy Najimy and her now-husband, Dan Finnerty.)

Melissa and Julie and Kathy and Dan are just two examples of the alternative, highly functional, family-oriented couples in the world today. Their children are thriving, and so are they. Love is love, and children can feel it if it's real. They're not interested, nor do they understand or care, if their family is traditional or not.

A Place to Call Home

In cases of private citizens who adopt children, parental information can remain their own business, and it's up to each couple to handle this as they see fit. In *Love, Ellen* I related the story of a child I heard about in North Carolina. He is African-American and his dads, whom I met, are white. It's obvious that he is adopted. When his friends ask him about it he says, "I have a birth mother, but I don't know her, so I have two dads instead. OK?"

When I spoke in Minneapolis not long ago, I met a lesbian couple who have two children and who have created a unique and loving family for them. The father is a friend of theirs, and he and his partner are very much a part of the children's upbringing. The men have the children on weekend nights, and once a week the two couples get together to discuss parenting issues and to just spend time together. One of the women told me that a highlight of the children's year is the local gay pride parade. Proud and happy about having parents who care so much about them, the children love to march in the parade. In fact, they often bring neighborhood friends along to march with them.

Adoption

I recently had a conversation with Dr. Jim Gordon in which he told me, "Over the years I have heard a lot of people refer to their deceased parents in a kind of wistful, wishful way. They'll say things like, 'Well, I think Dad loved me...he never kicked me out of the house.' Or 'Mom wasn't very good at expressing how she felt about me.' It occurs to me that you probably don't and won't hear too many children of gay parents saying things like that. Instead, these kids hear over and over again how much their parents love them and how much they care. Gay and lesbian parents have usually gone through so much to have or adopt children, they are very, very happy to have and love them. The children usually feel this love. These children may have other problems, but wondering whether they are loved won't be one of them."

Of course, adopted children often bring their own sensitivities into a family—ones that must be handled with great insight by their parents, whether those parents are gay or straight. Being adopted has many ramifications, the primary ones dealing with all the issues that surround rejection. Sooner or later a child is bound to ask herself why she was given away. Was there something wrong with me? Am I defective? Aren't I lovable enough to keep? If I'm not a good girl, will my adoptive parents give me away too?

Questions like these are not indictments against the adoptive mothers or fathers, nor are they indications that the children don't want to be with them. Adoptive parents have nothing to do with an adopted child's rejection anxieties. But they have everything to do with assuring the child that they will love him or her no matter what— and that there is nothing that child could ever say or do that would cause him or her to be given away. Needless to say, these feelings apply to all adoptions, not just adoptions by gay parents.

In addition to children's anxieties, it's important to keep in mind that parents too can have anxieties about adoption—about whether their children will one day reject them or want to seek out their biological parents. Obviously, gay and lesbian parents go through a lot to have or adopt children. Furthermore, they carry the extra baggage of social scrutiny and emotional pressure that heterosexual parents do not. Given these circumstances, there's a good chance gay couples may also carry a hypersensitivity about being rejected by their children that goes beyond the normal concerns of adoptive parents.

A Period of Adjustment

Beyond the issues of adoption, gay parents have a special challenge in introducing their children to the unique makeup of their family. Some episodes of *Ellen* dealt with Ellen's partner, Laurie, who had a daughter. I've

been told that these true-to-life situations were helpful
not only to the children of gay couples, but also to their
friends at school and in the neighborhood—giving everyone an opportunity to understand and redefine their concept of family.

An especially poignant story about a lesbian and her
son can be seen in *Serving in Silence*, the moving Glenn
Close film made Col. Grethe Cammermeyer. This
extraordinary woman was decorated with a Bronze Star
for her 14 months of service as a nurse in Vietnam and
went on to earn a Ph.D. from the University of
Washington and become chief nurse in the Washington
State National Guard. After 23 years of exceptional service to her country, this outstanding soldier was asked to
leave the U.S. Army because she is a lesbian. The Army
stated, "Homosexuality is incompatible with military
service."

Cammermeyer objected to her dismissal and sued the
Army. In the middle of her trial, one of Grethe's three
sons asked to move in with her instead of continuing to
live with his dad. However, the boy was afraid that his
presence in his Mom's house might be a problem—"your
not liking guys and all," he said to his mother.

Understanding that her son was afraid that she didn't
like men in general and him in particular, Colonel
Cammermeyer hugged her son and said, "My sexual ori-

entation has nothing to do with you. I love you for who are. So please don't stereotype me like that."

Confusions such as that of Grethe's son often emerge when a parent comes out of the closet. What's important to remember is that these misunderstandings can be cleared up. The critical issue here is staying sensitive to your child's feelings and trying to answer the questions he or she might have before the questions become obstacles to having an open, honest, and loving relationship.

A Positive Understanding

I recently met a woman whose partner is a trauma-room surgeon. The couple has a ten-year-old daughter who wants to be a civil rights attorney when she grows up. I was delighted when I met the daughter and saw that she was wearing a button with a picture of two women holding a baby. The caption read: "We are a family."

One of the things gay couples can do for their kids is to find other families with similar makeups. It always helps to know that you aren't alone. Obviously, your chances of connecting with other gay families are greater in large cities than in small towns. But if it's possible, socializing and talking over problems together can go a long way in offering comfort and validation as well as pleasure to these families.

In January 2000 I spoke in Jacksonville, Fla., where three darling little girls, ten to 12 years old, sat in the first row. During the question-and-answer period, one stood up and told me about a group they belong to called Children of Lesbians and Gays Everywhere (COLAGE). I later learned that the group meets once a month, and the children decide on an activity such as swimming, skating, or bowling. They can share and talk over any problems they might be having and, in general, be part of a wonderful support group.

This was the first I had heard of this organization, but I hope there will soon be chapters in many cities all over the country. If you are interested, the Web site address for information is COLAGE.org.

Another thing gay couples can do for their small children is to read them books and stories that deal with their situation. *Heather Has Two Mommies* by Lesléa Newman and *Daddy's Roommate* by Michael Willhoite are two children's books that can ease kids into an understanding of their family. It's no surprise that both of these works have been banned from certain libraries and schools throughout the country.

Books and support groups, other families and parental love—they all contribute to helping children embrace their own family as well as giving them the tools to cope as they move into the larger world of school and community. Our goal should be not only to teach our children to take these giant steps with confidence—but to take them with pride.

Chapter Seven

The Marriage Dilemma

Let me not to the marriage of true minds
Admit impediments.

—William Shakespeare

Doing the Expected

Beyond doing what is expected of them, gay men and women marry straight partners for a variety of reasons: they need the camouflage; they want to prove that they can conform to societal norms; they hope to live up to their parents' dreams for them or to change their orientation by changing their focus. Often gay people have submerged their feelings so completely, they don't even realize they are in denial. Such individuals view themselves as simply doing what society demands.

One woman I met recently told me that after 25 years of marriage, two children, and one grandchild, she finally came out as a lesbian.

"When I was young I knew I wanted to have children, and I thought being married to a man was the only way to do it," she said. Gradually, she came to terms with her homosexuality. Her eyes twinkled when she told me, "I should have known I was gay. In kindergarten I remember hiding in the bushes and whistling at the other little girls as they passed by."

I've heard of two instances of young people who had never confronted the fact that they were gay, even though they were in their 20s. In both cases, after they became engaged, they each met that special someone—and called off the engagement.

One young man I talked to in Atlanta when I was on my book tour for *Love, Ellen* told me that when he broke his heterosexual engagement, he returned home to England to tell his parents in person. His parents had a family tradition of giving each child a set of china when they married. Later, when he told his parents he had fallen deeply in love with a same-sex partner, they still gave him his set of china. His eyes brimmed with tears as he told me this story.

A young woman named Susan told me a story that would be funny if it weren't so sad. Her parents know she's gay, but they deny it—and she plays right along with them. Susan has been engaged three times. The last time she had chosen 12 bridesmaids, all of whom had bought their gowns, and her parents had rented a huge ballroom for the reception. A few days before the wedding, though, Susan once again called the whole thing off. Susan's mother still insists that her daughter's lesbianism is just a phase.

Coming Out of a Marriage

After they've been married, the challenge for thousands of gay people is how to get out of that marriage with children, ex-spouse, and family emotionally intact. This process is predominantly a present-day phenomenon.

It goes without saying that when you have children, coming out of the closet at the same time you come out of a marriage is a nightmare of dilemmas. I asked my friend Dr. Jim Gordon for his advice on what gay parents should tell their children when their heterosexual marriages end.

"We're the pioneers," Jim says. "We have to set the pace. It's not something we were taught in school. The best advice is to tell your children the truth, without apologizing and without guilt. If you feel good about yourself, that will come through.

"I heard about one man," Jim says, "who has ended his marriage because he is gay, but he won't admit this to his ten-year-old son or allow him to meet his lover. This isn't a promising start for the son's acceptance of his father's homosexuality. I must add here, since I'm a firm believer in people coming out when they're ready, that this dad has the same right; however, honesty does seem to be the best policy within families."

Jim's feeling is that if kids see a weak spot, they'll jump on it and use it the rest of their lives. Seeing or not seeing a weakness may be one explanation for why some children are completely accepting of their parent's orientation and why others are resentful and judgmental. This has to do with approaching the issue from a proactive rather than a reactive stance.

"Use honesty and common sense," Jim says, "telling your child what is appropriate for him to know at his age. And above all, tell him you love him the same as you always did. No difference."

By now I've heard family stories that range from complete endorsement to outright rejection. In one family I know about, a mother's daughter is totally accepting of her and her partner, while her son is not. Sometimes a male child of a lesbian mother assumes that his mom doesn't like men and therefore doesn't like him. This misunderstanding can cause a rift that must be dealt with in a prompt, honest, and forthright manner. The son's insecurity, anger, and sense of rejection should not be allowed to fester. If the son is willing, therapy can be useful in cases such as this.

Truth and Consequences

The combination of coming out and coming out of a marriage reconfigures the world of the family and turns a child's world upside down. No one can predict what will happen when you take this giant step. Change walks hand in hand with risk, and all we can do in life is do our best. When you reveal yourself to your children, it is inevitable that some kids are going to behave negatively and some will behave positively. Sometimes, in spite of your best efforts and intentions, the response you get is completely unpredictable. Some kids will shift into denial and confusion. Some will be filled with rage or retreat into silence. And others—such as the young woman who had recently learned that her mother is gay—take the change in stride. "I love my mother," she told me when I met her after one of my speeches. "And she happens to be gay. People should just get over it."

Unexpected Turn in the Road

Although this young woman seemed to take her mother's coming out in stride, the time immediately surrounding separation or divorce is generally a period of great upheaval for all concerned. As is true with coming out in general, married gay men and women have probably been struggling with their sexuality for years—perhaps even all their lives. Sometimes the spouse is aware that something is wrong and may even be able to pinpoint the problem. *E! News Daily* host Steve Kmetko told *The Advocate* magazine that it was his wife who finally told him he was gay. Less frequently, either for reasons of ignorance or denial, the spouse doesn't have a clue. Either way, the ramifications of a pending split are momentous.

I know of one woman named Lorrie who was married for 15 years to a man named Carl. Her husband was a piece of work—cranky, angry, and self-involved. He wasn't all bad, however, because when Lorrie wanted to go away to a special graduate school in a distant city, Carl was in favor of her decision. It could be that he was just a decent fellow and wanted to support his wife. It could be that Carl wanted the cat away so he could play. Or it could be that he just wanted some relief from a difficult marriage. Whatever his motivations, Carl and Lorrie arranged it so that their teenage sons could spend time with both of them while she was away at school.

Then came the big "oops." Immersed in school and intrigued by her studies, Lorrie went to a graduate department party one night and fell in love with the mother of a fellow student.

Eventually Lorrie got a divorce and moved in with her new lover. You can imagine how her husband and sons felt about this. Carl was enraged at the betrayal and humiliated that his wife had left him for a woman. And the sons were confused and angry. The boys' interpretation of the affair was that their mother had rejected men and in so doing had rejected them.

It took years of therapy and professional support for the husband to accept what had happened and for the sons to adjust to it. Today, Lorrie and her boys are as close as she hoped they would be. One son is happily married, and the other is comfortable with himself and excelling in his job. The children of both women get along, and their former husbands have come to accept the situation.

Restoring peace and tranquillity to all their lives wasn't easy. But living without it was not an option. Eventually everyone involved came to understand that they were all better off than they were before. The countless hours of effort and determination paid off.

The Straight Truth

When families are disrupted by divorce, counseling can always be helpful. When the divorce is complicated by the involvement of children and the fact that one of the spouses is gay, counseling is essential.

Unfortunately, when married gay men and women realize they can no longer live the lie, they and their children aren't the only ones who suffer. The straight husband or wife must come to grips with the news that their marriage, which may have seemed relatively "normal," is ending. They must also accept the fact that their husband or wife is gay. A double whammy!

There are probably more support groups for gay people than straight ones. I know of only one support group for straight people with gay spouses (or gay former spouses). Straight Spouse Network is an international support group of heterosexual spouses and partners. Its mission is to "reach out, heal, [and] build bridges." This is an admirable and vital organization that can help everyone in the family adjust to their new reality. The group can be reached on the Web at ssnetwk.org.

The Great Debate: Should I or Shouldn't I?

As with coming out of the closet, coming out of a marriage is a highly individual process. With a national divorce rate of 25% to 50% (50% in California) we know that most marriages—even the best ones—experience rocky times. No doubt, many gay men and women leave troubled marriages and only later admit to themselves that they are gay. A friend of mine did just that, and he's certainly not alone.

If you're one of those people debating about how and when to get out of your bad marriage, my advice would be to do so sooner rather than later. I can speak from personal experience that the longer you stay in a bad marriage, the more corrosive the relationship becomes.

I pretended I was happy in both my marriages for years, staying far beyond the time when either relationship had any meaning. With 20-20 hindsight, I might have done things differently. However, when you're in the situation—with all the emotional turmoil of the moment—you just do the best you can.

Realistically, if you are gay and in a marriage in which you love your husband or wife, it is insulting to stay in the relationship. Your spouse deserves to know the truth. He or she deserves the respect of knowing that honesty in your marriage takes precedence over deceit.

In all likelihood, if you are gay, your spouse senses your ambivalence. After all, sexual accommodation can only go so far. Faking it is one thing. Living a lie all the time is another. It is insulting to your spouse to continue to deceive. And the longer you wait, the more both your spirits suffer.

I have spoken to lots of children who had gay parents locked in straight marriages. Many of these kids tell me that once they got over the shock of learning the truth about their mother or father, they were able to accept their gay parent. Time, the most reliable healer of all, mended their emotional wounds. And love mended their spirits.

I saw a wonderful example of this recently when I attended a Human Rights Campaign dinner in St. Louis. After dinner I was introduced to a young man named Glen. He isn't gay, but his father is. This fine young man not only accepts his father, but also actively participates in the fight for equal rights for gays and lesbians. Glen took part in the local vigil for Matthew Shepard and had organized an antiviolence rally on his college campus. He asked if I'd put in a word about it during my speech, and I was more than happy to do so.

At the same dinner I met a beautiful young woman who said she was married and had three children before she came to terms with her sexual orientation. In telling me her story, she said that after she came out, watching *Ellen* became mandatory in their home. The show helped her kids accept their new family situation. It also helped them understand more about their mother.

Sadly, not all family transitions are that smooth. There are many children who cannot or will not accept the change in their parents. And many parents who cannot or will not accept the change in their children. When this happens, everyone loses. When left unmended, the separation becomes an ongoing tragedy—one that leaves deep and abiding scars.

When a rift such as this occurs, my best advice is to keep trying to build a bridge to reconciliation, no matter how hopeless the situation seems. There's always a possibility that the parents or children who have done the rejecting will begin to see that life is painted in shades of gray instead of black and white. They might come to understand and accept the inevitable. Give everyone the gift of time. As Anne can attest, change can happen. And so can miracles.

The Definitions of Marriage

One of my favorite stories about marriage and families concerns a ten-year-old girl named Lisa. When she and her classmates were asked to draw a family picture, Lisa drew a picture of her grandmother and her girlfriend. This loving couple meant family to her.

Viewed through the eyes of an innocent child, marriage took on new meaning. What wasn't so clear to Lisa

144 / Betty DeGeneres

Betty DeGeneres

At dinner celebrating my birthday in 1997.

was what her "grandmothers" should call each other.

I think it's interesting to hear how gay couples refer to each other. Comedian and activist Kate Clinton makes fun of the term "partner," saying it sounds too much like a square dance—"swing your partner, do-si-do." Anne and Ellen call each other "wife." And two men I know refer to each other as "husband." They're in committed, loving relationships, and that's how they think of each other. Some couples prefer the term "lover." My friends Rob and David, who have been together 13 years, prefer "boyfriend." " 'Lover' has a sexual connotation," Rob told me, "and that's what we're trying to get away from. Our relationship is about so much more than that—especially after 13 years!" Others in long-term relationships settle for the term "life partner."

Along with the struggle for equal rights for gays and lesbians, marriage to a same-sex partner is very much in the forefront of religious and political discussion these days. With the laudable exception of Reform rabbis and some Episcopal priests, most leaders are afraid of dealing with the problem in an honest, straightforward way. Clergymen either decry the idea as the work of the devil or embrace it as a manifestation of God's love. Politicians take one look at the subject and either remain silent or use the possibility of gay marriage as a cause célèbre to further their political ambitions.

In light of the fact that few people in public life want to condone the possibility of same-sex marriage, some couples I've talked to say they will settle for the term "domestic partnership" or "civil union." *Settle for* is the key phrase here. Others complain that "separate but equal" status is never equal. African-Americans can certainly attest to that.

Those who are gay—or those of us who have loved

ones who are gay—are sometimes surprised at the ignorance of the general public on this subject. I was staying
at a Nashville hotel in February of 1999 and talking with
a parking valet while I waited for my car. He asked where
I was going, and I told him to a Human Rights Campaign
event. That led to an explanation about the work I'm
doing. I told him about two men I had just met who had
been together 35 years and have no legal rights. I told
him that without specific legal documents, gay men and
women cannot make medical decisions for each other.
They cannot inherit property. They cannot be considered
members of each other's immediate family in a medical
emergency. They cannot include their partner on their
medical insurance. They cannot get other benefits, such
as tax write-offs, travel discounts, and family memberships. In most states gay couples cannot adopt children.
And they cannot get the public respect for their relationship that is commonly afforded to married couples.

"But gay people can get married in some states,"
he said.

I quickly corrected him.

"I think they can get married in Texas," he said.

Again, I corrected him.

Needless to say, the subject of marriage not only
evokes ignorance, it evokes hostility.

It always amuses me when I hear right-wing religious

leaders talk about the horrors of gay marriage. In the next breath they discuss the "gay lifestyle," usually implying that homosexuals are promiscuous and that they should do something about it. I'd think these twisted souls would approve of an arrangement in which homosexuals make a legal and loving commitment to one partner so that the so-called promiscuity the far right condemns might not be such an issue.

As far as I'm concerned, it makes perfect sense for gay people to be married. I know Anne and Ellen will take that step when it becomes legal. Why shouldn't they? They share a household and all the responsibilities that entails. They consult each other on all decisions, and in all respects they are in a committed, lifelong relationship. Of course it should be validated by law. And when that day comes I'll be a happy and enthusiastic mother of the brides.

Homosexuals are taxpaying citizens and as such should be entitled to the same rights, responsibilities, and benefits as other Americans are. If particular ministers, priests, or rabbis don't want to perform the service, no one will force them to do it. There are plenty of enlightened, gay-friendly clergy who are willing to marry gay couples. There is also the option of going before a judge or justice of the peace.

When the day comes that gay couples can be married,

it will be a giant step toward the recognition and validation of gay relationships. It will also encourage all those
family values of love and trust and commitment that the
religious right is so concerned about. And aren't we all!

To Have and to Hold

Many gay and lesbian couples have marriage cere-
monies, even though the ritual gives them no status in
the eyes of the law. In spite of the social obstacles, the
couples want to celebrate their love and declare their
intentions before God, their families, and their friends.

A new book called *The Wedding: A Family's Coming
Out Story* by Douglas Wythe and Andrew Merling, and
Andrew's parents, Roslyn and Sheldon Merling,
describes in detail what a gay couple and their families
go through in reaching this decision and actually getting
to that joyous day.

My good friend Rob said to me, "I've noticed an interesting dynamic. When I meet old friends they say, 'Are
you still with David?' They wouldn't ask that if we were
married. After 13 years they'd just say, 'How's David?' "
He's right. Gay couples are systematically deprived of the
aura of permanence and the automatic respect that marriage confers. And that, as I used to say as a child, just
isn't fair.

The Enlightened Exception

In a ruling that opens the door to a more enlightened and inclusive attitude toward gay couples, the state of Vermont recently sanctioned the concept of a "civil union" between same-sex couples. This isn't marriage—which is still defined by the state as a union between a man and a woman—but it does officially provide to gay couples the spousal rights that married couples already enjoy.

This means that the rights of married couples as defined by state law—concerning family leave, inheritance, insurance coverage, child custody, medical decisions—are extended to those gay couples who obtain a license from their town clerk and who are certified by a judge, a member of the clergy, or a justice of the peace. It also means that if the couple splits up, they would have to file for dissolution of the union.

Although many people are preparing to man the barricades against similar laws that might be passed in other states, others are celebrating the victory. They are also hoping that once people understand that this law does not weaken the institution of marriage, other states might follow Vermont's lead and adopt a more family-friendly attitude toward gay couples.

Home Sweet Home

The fight for equal rights has taken up most of the
energy for gay causes. This being the case, few people
have looked at what happens to gay people—singles and
couples—when they grow old.

Just the other day I heard of a remarkable organization
called the Gay and Lesbian Association of Retiring
Persons. I E-mailed GLARP at glarp@earthlink.net to
ask about the organization. I got the following reply
from a woman named Veronica St. Claire. I'm quoting
from her letter verbatim because she states their case so
clearly.

*My partner (of 18 years), Mary Thorndal, and I formed
the Gay and Lesbian Association of Retiring Persons, a
nonprofit 501c(3) public purpose organization, in 1996.
We have backgrounds in law, psychology, business, and
Mary has a medical background—she was a nurse in
Vietnam and taught psychiatric nursing at the University
of Arizona before becoming a lawyer. Some personal experiences of friends who needed care—one had medication
management problems, the other a kidney transplant—
made us believe that with the advance of lesbian and gay
rights in the '90s, the time had come for a gay and lesbian-
friendly retirement facility.*

Actually, when we started we sent out a one-page survey to find out what persons in our community who were getting older, wanted. We thought GLARP would be like a G/L AARP, but immediately we got responses asking for senior housing.

As you know, many in our community have no family at all or are estranged; many have been married—I have three adult children and only my son relates to us; my two daughters do not—so one needs to gather in the family that is around, we thought. We also realized that that kind of housing wouldn't be limited to GLBTs but also to persons who had lesbians and gays in their families and would want to retire to be near them....

We are planning a retirement community in a village concept, of 100–200 units of independent and assisted units with a skilled component either on the property or adjacent to it. We have a full team (LGBT and straight) of planners, architects, business advisers—and plan a joint venture with an East Coast development company, one of whose partners is a gay man whose dream (like ours) is to create such a community....

We have made a number—lots, in fact—of grant applications but with limited success. We feel that once we have done a project, then the gates will be open. In the meantime, GLARP has been funded by us personally, by memberships, some donations, and a few grants. But we have kept the organization small and focused on our goal—to develop senior housing. The nonprofit entity will ensure that whatever we do will stay in the community after we are gone, and we have ensured continuity by bringing in a board member who was 29 when we started and [who] has been involved closely ever since.

All of Veronica's information made me think about the gay men and women who are now in retirement homes that may be not only unfriendly toward homosexuals but openly hostile. That there is a need for a retirement center such as the one described is an understatement, to say the least.

Veronica went on to say that their facility will be in Cathedral City, near Palm Springs, Calif. One can only wish them the greatest success so that people will be encouraged to build similar facilities all over the country. Most of us spend all our lives looking for a place called home. This need becomes critical when we are elderly. It's time we created this special place for gay people as well as straight ones. We all deserve this final kindness.

Chapter Eight

Religion—Who's Right?

We have just enough religion to make us hate, but not
enough to make us love one another.
                                        —Jonathan Swift

Religion: Beauty and the Beast

On one of the many trips I've taken in the last few years, I was being driven to the airport and struck up a conversation with the driver, who happened to be African-American. He was excited to know that I'm Ellen's mom, saying he admires her talent and admires her for speaking up.

The more I told him about what I'm doing and why, the more I could see he had a problem with the subject. He kept asking, "What about people who go by what the Bible says?"

I answered that with my usual: The Bible has been used to justify slavery, to justify women not having the right to vote, and to justify laws against mixed marriages. I asserted that there are no second-class citizens in the United States and that we all deserve equal rights.

By the time we got to the airport, the taxi driver, at the very least, had some new ideas to mull over. He had picked me up at 6:30 A.M. As I got out of the car I said, "I'll bet you didn't know you'd have such a serious discussion this early in the day." He agreed and we both laughed.

I think it would go a long way toward ending the divisiveness in this country if there could be friendly, low-key conversations like this all over this country—especially about religion! My opinion is that no matter how literally or strictly you interpret the Bible, this does not give you the right to deny basic rights to a group of people who don't live their lives according to your interpretation of the Bible.

I consider myself to be a religious person. And I respect the spiritual grace that so many people bring into their lives—whether they are Christian, Buddhist,

Jewish, Muslim, or anything else. Personally, I have always read the Bible, and I have always tried to live a good and charitable life. This includes not only tolerating difference, but also celebrating it.

Shortly after Ellen came out, I was on a national radio show talking about gays and lesbians when a listener called in from Arizona and asked, "Why have you forsaken God and our Lord Jesus Christ?"

"Excuse me," I said, "but I never said that I did. You're assuming that because I don't interpret the Bible in the same way you do that I have forsaken God."

Nothing could be further from the truth.

It never ceases to astonish me when I hear followers of fundamentalist religion using quotes from the Bible to justify scapegoating those who are different.

Casting the First Stone

I used to think that pointing at evildoers was how we identified and defined evil. But I've come to understand that why we place blame, and the way we do it, is much more complex than that. Accusing others of a sin is an unconscious but common way of deflecting attention from the same sin in ourselves. This being the case, what we choose to condemn in others reveals more about us than we probably want people to know.

Scapegoating is a common psychological phenomenon routinely used on a personal, political, and national level. Carl Jung, the esteemed philosopher and psychoanalyst, said, "Only that which we cannot accept within ourselves do we find impossible to live with in others." He also said that scapegoating is used when we want to avoid our own flaws; that we deny our own darkness by projecting it onto others.

Hermann Hesse, recipient of the Nobel Prize for Literature, echoes this when he says, "If you hate a person, you hate something in him that is part of yourself. What isn't part of ourselves doesn't disturb us."

And M. Scott Peck, the eminent psychiatrist and best-selling author, says that while scapegoaters "seem to lack any motivation to *be* good, they intensely desire to appear good." I have only to think of all these Christ-professing, God-fearing, gay-hating "Christians" to understand what he's saying. And I wonder if the day will ever come when we stop pointing our fingers at what we hate most in ourselves.

Leviticus: The Source and the Shame

Christians who are opposed to equal rights for homosexuals quote tirelessly from Leviticus, apparently convinced that if they repeat the words often enough, their tedious repetition will close down all argument on the point they are trying to make.

These pseudo pious people only choose one verse to quote—the one they agree with: "Thou shall not lie with mankind as with womankind: It is abomination." They recite this single verse ad nauseum. They manage to overlook the rest. They don't quote other verses in Leviticus about not "mingling fibers," about putting to death everyone that "curseth his father or his mother," about putting adulterers and adulteresses to death, about putting to death a man or a woman with a "familiar spirit."

It should be noted also that back in the time of Leviticus, people had an unusual take on their fellow men with physical defects. Apparently the Lord told Moses to tell Aaron that if a man "hath a blemish; he shall not come nigh to offer the offerings of the Lord." That included "a blind man, or a lame, or he that hath a flat nose, or any thing superfluous, or a man that is bro- ken-footed, or broken-handed, or crookbacked, or a dwarf, or that hath a blemish in his eye, or be scurvy, or scabbed."

Beyond all that, it's important to keep in mind that Leviticus also asks people to "love thy neighbor as thy- self" and not to avenge or "bear any grudge against the children of thy people."

2500 years make a difference. That same distance in understanding should include the fact that there is so much more to homosexuality than a "man lying with a man or a woman lying with a woman." Homosexuality is about love and commitment.

That Was Then and This Is Now

When we talk about the Old Testament, we sometimes forget that we're talking about a time when priests did everything they could to increase the numbers of their tribes—hence the stringent rules about what people could and could not do; what they could and could not eat. Certainly, lying with someone of the same sex wouldn't contribute to the population growth, which is why the priests might have defined this act as abomination.

It's a mystery to me why present-day religions pick and choose ancient laws to adhere to. Even literalists can't possibly take every single word of the Bible literally.

There are so many beautiful commands and promises in the Bible. One of my favorite verses in the Old Testament is from Micah 6:8. "He hath shewed thee, O man, what is good; and what doth the Lord require of thee, but to do justly, and to love mercy, and to walk humbly with thy God?" To me, that verse is all about my taking responsibility for myself—no judging of others, no condemning. I have plenty to do just trying to be fair, merciful, and humble.

In the New Testament, all of Jesus' teachings were about blessings—all the "Blessed are ye's" of the Beatitudes—and about inclusion and nonjudgment. His message is about who you should love, not who you should hate.

Joseph Campbell said the god you worship is the god you deserve. I could add that many people worship the god they've been taught to worship. Many gay men and women are staunch adherents of their religions—they are Catholic, Protestant, Jewish, Muslim, and even members of some fundamentalist churches and temples. It's difficult for me, however, to understand how gay members of fundamentalist religious organizations can justify participating in a church that routinely reviles who they are.

I suppose people's religion—and the God they worship in that particular theology—is such a powerful part of their past that they cannot envision a present or future without it. But I still question their support. I even wonder if a component of their worship might be tied up in denying their self-worth—in refusing to believe that they are deserving enough to walk away from people and places that demean their essence and diminish their spirit.

Having said that, I do know that there are individual churches and synagogues within these religions that embrace their members who happen to be gay. Last year I was in Boston on Palm Sunday and attended mass at a Catholic church with my dear friend Harry. In this church gay men and women make up the majority of the congregation, and I don't know when I've felt such joy in a religious gathering. All these people celebrating the miracle of Christ's life together under one welcoming roof created an atmosphere of love that was palpable.

After the service, Harry introduced me to a nun, and I commented on the loving atmosphere I felt everywhere I turned.

"We can hardly get people out of here to go home," she said. "They all want to stay and have coffee and talk."

Harry also told me that this church has a tremendous charitable outreach program for the surrounding community. No doubt about it, the members of this church—gay and straight—are living the meaning of brotherhood and love.

Anne and Ellen recently acquired a wonderful book of photographs called *Century*. In it, a picture from 1920 shows 900 gallons of wine being poured down a drain in Los Angeles. The caption called prohibition "a fit of American Puritanism." What an apt phrase. I think it precisely describes the hue and cry of the religious right

today. They're trying to take us back to the Puritan period when everyone had to think alike and those who
didn't were punished.

Neo-Pilgrims Among Us

During question-and-answer periods in my speeches,
when questions about fundamentalist Christians and
their literal interpretations of the Bible arise, I've often
referred to them as Puritans.

Patricia Nell Warren, well-known author of *The
Front Runner* and a number of other books, has coined
the term "neo-Pilgrims." She has very generously
shared with me her forthcoming book called *Neo-
Pilgrims Among Us: The True History of Religious
Liberty in the U.S.*

In this exhaustively researched work, Patricia states:

*Today some Americans believe that all the persecuted
Protestant sects who came to the New World had some
wonderful sweeping vision of "religious liberty for all." Not
so. Way too much of the stuff we read about colonial times
romanticizes things or gilds them. Many of these Protestant
refugees were fiercely intolerant of others and interpreted
any need for "liberty" as applying only to themselves. The
concept of "liberty for all" struggled slowly, painfully, into*

existence like a butterfly out of its chrysalis....

Yet there were still Americans who passionately believed that "God" (as defined by them) commanded them to protect religion through civil government. They would not easily give up their perceived right to override the consciences of others. Henceforth they would regard American "liberalism" as their deadly enemy. I call these people "neo-Pilgrims," regardless of what church they might belong to, because they are still around today and share a common nostalgia for colonial established religion.

The specter of history repeating itself with "neo-Pilgrims" insisting that their interpretation of the Bible is the only acceptable one (i.e., Southern Baptists trying to convert Mormons and Jews) is frightening indeed.

I've known lots of people forced to leave a religious tradition they love in order to find the solace of community and prayer in a church or temple that welcomes them without judgment. These havens are increasing in number across the country. Los Angeles has numerous churches, as well as two Jewish temples, that don't ask their members to discard their identities at the door.

If you feel more comfortable worshipping in a gay community, you can seek out the Metropolitan Community Church in your area. Founded by Reverend Troy Perry when he was excommunicated from his fundamentalist denomination for declaring his homosexuality, this church is now not only national but international and has become a loving refuge for gay communicants. These are just a few examples of many churches and synagogues that welcome gay people into their midst.

We Are the World

When I was making notes for this book and what I would want to include in it, I read a wonderful piece in *The Los Angeles Times* by Charles Watson about acceptance. His final paragraphs read:

We may be Christians, Jews, Muslims, Buddhists, Atheists, Agnostics, or Hindus. We may be males, females or even transgendered. We may be heterosexuals, bisexuals, homosexuals, or transsexuals. And we may be black, Latino, white, Asian, Indian, or a host of other ethnic categories. In fact, we may each identify ourselves in ways that are both separate and the same in many different categories and experiences.

On one end of the spectrum we all are the same: human. On the other end we are all unique: there is no one just like us, even a genetic clone.

But more importantly, we all exist together in families, neighborhoods, circles of friends, work groups and com-

Jill Shafer

On the job—speaking at schools and corporations about acceptance of
diversity and about loving our children unconditionally. Simple, isn't it?
This particular stop was at Wilmington College in Wilmington, Ohio.

munities that are defined by geographic proximity or sim-
ilarity or even virtual communities defined by common
interest.

In the end we must find a way to embrace unity without
uniformity and diversity without divisiveness.

I love this writer's plea for the acceptance of diversity. Certainly there is diversity throughout the world. There is diversity within the gay community. Anne and Ellen are perfect examples of this. In some ways, they couldn't be more different. And yet it is those very differences that contribute to the creation of the loving bond that exists between them.

Of course, it's important for us to learn to live with the differences among us. But we need to do more than that. We need to learn to embrace that difference with an open and loving heart. Until we do that, we will continue—as individuals and as citizens of the world—to live in an atmosphere of hatred and strife. God willing, the day will come soon when we can celebrate "diversity without divisiveness."

Expanding Your Family

Another way to express diversity without divisiveness is in how we celebrate our families. These days millions of people face the need to create their own family. This happens for a variety of reasons. Living in our mobile society, they might find themselves hundreds or thousands of miles from blood relatives. They may be alone in the world because they don't have any living relatives. Or, for a variety of reasons, they may have been rejected by their families.

Frequently the reason for rejection is the family member's sexual orientation. As I mentioned earlier, in his book *Prayer Warriors* Stuart Miller tells a harrowing story of how his family rejected him because he was gay. His parents and their troglodytic church condemned him as a disgusting sodomite for his "deathstyle choice." To make certain he got the message, Stuart's sister wrote to him about God's wrath, saying this supposedly loving and benevolent spirit would either "change you or kill you."

As a result of stories such as Stuart's, it is not uncommon to find tightly knit gay "families" in cities throughout the country. Often they involve PFLAG parents and gay men and women. The PFLAG moms and dads are only too happy to act as surrogate parents to men and women whose families have turned their backs on them.

Another example of creative families can be seen in Helen and Lynne, two women in a small town who started a lesbian pride parade nine years ago. They began with a grand total of five women. Last year 60 women marched. I asked if they couldn't let gay men march with them. Helen said, "No, we just want to celebrate gay women in this one. We march on the sidewalk downtown, and gay men and our friends clap and cheer. Then we cross to the other side of the street, and they cross and clap and cheer over there." Lynne added, "We have a brunch at our house afterward, and last year 80 women came." She paused, then added, "Everybody can't be 'out.' "

Helen has two grown children by her previous marriage, and now a grandchild. She said her son and daughter are very accepting. In fact, her son said he wishes he could find a girlfriend like Lynne.

In their continuing quest to support and celebrate lesbians, Helen and Lynne's home has become a haven to women who need a place of refuge. Some, fleeing an angry husband, stay a few days. Others, wounded by the rejection of a family that no longer wants anything to do with them, have stayed as long as five months. Their core support group—better yet, their family—has been together nine years.

Created Families: Old and New

Not far from where I live, there's still another model of family energy at work in a group of senior citizen lesbians. The women have been close friends for more than 20 years. They travel together, celebrate holidays and birthdays together, even consult with the group when any of them has to make a major decision. Loving, caring, protecting—this sounds like family to me!

In my travels I recently met a young man named Dudley who told me about five men who went to a prominent Ivy League college together. They were friends throughout their college years, although they all lived in the closet. After they graduated, they came out one by one. As it turned out, Dudley says, three of the men ended up in Los Angeles. These men and their partners have formed their own kind of family. They spend holidays together. They also celebrate birthdays and travel together. Even though none of them have been outright rejected by their families, they have not been embraced with the support and love that children should be able to expect from their mothers and fathers.

"My friends and I—we're family in every sense of the word," Dudley says.

And just the other day I heard a great story from a man who raised his daughter with his partner. She is now married and has a baby of her own. There are three sets of grandparents—the husband's parents, the wife's mother and her new husband, and the wife's father and his partner. Not long ago the daughter told her dad that she and her husband talked about who they would want to raise their child if anything happened to them. They both chose her dad and his partner.

When we choose our families there is often a level of support and compatibility that doesn't exist in a natural family. In the days before Ellen was on TV, when she was on the comedy circuit, I once heard a comedian say,

"Would you visit your family if they weren't your family?" A funny but thought-provoking question. Some of today's gay and lesbian families might enthusiastically answer, "Yes!"

In created families, men and women are there because they want to be, not because they have to be. And they are bound by a common outlook, a common purpose, and a common love.

A Final Word

In this book I've talked about family, about what it means and how it enriches our lives. Families all over the world include straight, gay, lesbian, bisexual, and trans-gendered people—whether they are recognized and embraced or not. Gays, lesbians, bisexual individuals, and transgendered people are our mothers, fathers, sons, daughters, sisters, brothers, aunts, uncles, cousins—even our grandparents. This is a fact, and it isn't going away.

I've also talked about coming out and the dire results of keeping secrets from one another. Yes, I know we all have secrets. Kate doesn't know who her father is. Jack's sister is an alcoholic. And Sammy's father beat his mother. Those are facts that you may or may not want to reveal. But in the deepest part of me, I am convinced that keeping secrets about our most fundamental self, our God-given spirit, not only diminishes our life, it diminishes the lives of others—depriving us of our right to be who we are, and depriving those around us of the opportunity to grow in compassion and expand in understanding.

Whether it is our life or the life of a son or daughter, honoring who we are lends purpose to our days, meaning to our relationships, and grace to our lives. And when our courage fails and our hearts grow faint, the words of the Apostle John can bring comfort to us all: The truth shall make you free.

Afterword

I had already turned this book in to my publisher when the Millennium March on Washington took place on April 30, 2000. The night before the march, the Human Rights Campaign presented the Equality Rocks concert at RFK Stadium. Both events were life-changing for the thousands of people who attended. No one who was there can ever be complacent again about being gay or having a gay loved one.

The star-studded concert was a resounding success. My favorite memories are of George Michael singing an achingly romantic "I Remember You" with harp accompaniment, George Michael and Garth Brooks's duet of "Freedom," everything Melissa Etheridge did with her boundless energy, k.d. lang's splendid voice, and Tipper Gore on drums—what a great lady she is.

But the most special highlight for me was the ovation

Ellen received just from walking on stage. The thunderous applause rose in a roar then came in waves. And just when we thought it would die down, the crowd cheered even more. Both Ellen and I were stunned by the audience's reaction. When she came backstage, we hugged and broke into tears. The moment was overwhelming.

On another personal note, when Anne introduced the Pet Shop Boys, she spoke eloquently about being gay, and at the March the next day she spoke even more eloquently. At Dulles Airport Monday morning a woman approached me and said, "You know, I didn't know much about Anne before, but her speeches were amazing. She's so articulate."

I proudly replied, "She always is. I think thousands and thousands of people now know how wonderful she is."

On the day of the March, the speeches were certainly inspiring, but what was most inspiring was the hundreds of thousands of people, gay and straight, all just being what they are: families that love each other.

And that's what we're all about.